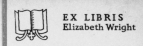
B.C.

GOD WHO ACTS

STUDIES IN BIBLICAL THEOLOGY

GOD WHO
ACTS

Biblical Theology
as Recital

G. ERNEST WRIGHT

SCM PRESS LTD
56 BLOOMSBURY STREET
LONDON

First published October 1952
Reprinted December 1954, *March* 1956

Printed in Great Britain by
Robert Cunningham and Sons Ltd.
Longbank Works, Alva

To
MY FATHER
from whom I have received a dissatisfaction
with every present; and

to
MY MOTHER
in whom was the patience and
self-effacement of her Lord

CONTENTS

PREFACE

THE purpose of this monograph is to describe the special and characteristic nature of the Biblical presentation of faith and to defend the use of the word 'theology' for it. This means, however, that the term must be rescued from the exclusive and private use of the systematic theologians. To most of them, as to most others, it has meant propositional dogmatics, stated as abstractly and universally as possible and arranged in accordance with a preconceived and coherent system. Obviously, the Bible contains nothing of the sort; in fact, its writers seem completely uninterested in this type of discussion. As a result, there has been a tendency to disparage the Bible and to assume that since it belongs to a pre-logical age, it cannot be allowed to speak in its own way. Instead, it must be systematized in some manner, else its witness for the modern Church will be ineffectual. But to systematize it has meant that one has attempted to organise its data by means of a pattern of thought foreign to its own nature: i.e., by means of the rubrics of propositional theology. Such procedure is a matter of great concern to the specialist in Biblical history because it so easily disregards the Biblical variety, change and flexibility. It is more Hellenic than Hebraic, and the heart of Biblical faith somehow eludes it.

The contention of the pages which follow is that Biblical theology, while it is not propositional and systematic dogmatics, is nevertheless a defensible entity of its own kind, one that should influence the work of contemporary theologians more profoundly than it thus far has done. It is a theology of recital or proclamation of the acts of God, together with the inferences drawn therefrom. These acts are themselves interpretations of historical events, or projections from known events to past and future, all described within the conceptual frame of one people in a certain historical continuum. The writer can make no claim for originality in the discovery of this fact. On the contrary, it is one with the meaning of which thinking people throughout the world Church are now struggling. A few theologians have made the point central in at least the first part of certain of their books, though as a rule it seems not to have been determinative of what is written in the remainder. The term 'mythology' has been revived as one means of dealing with this central characteristic of the Bible, and we are told that either the Scripture must be demythologized for the modern man, or else there must be careful explanation to the effect that the only way the human mind has of dealing with ultimate truth is in terms of myth. Consequently, it has become necessary to discuss this question in any treatment of Biblical theology, and with such a discussion the present volume ends.

The primary aim of this book, however, is not to enter upon a lengthy discussion of the relation between the Bible and contemporary theology. It is rather to indicate the nature of Biblical theology itself and in so doing to suggest a way out of the current dilemma of the Church and its scholars who seek to relate the historical and theological disciplines in Biblical study so that the Bible may play its proper role in the revival of evangelical theology. Yet before this can be done, it is necessary that the modern Church deal with the Old Testament in a more serious manner than it has yet done. Indeed, we find ourselves today in a position that makes it difficult to take the Old Testament seriously. Consequently, it seemed necessary to begin with this problem before proceeding to the main theme, because there can be no truly Biblical theology unless the two Testaments are held firmly together as the Bible of the Church.

The title for the book presented something of a problem because of the danger of misunderstanding what was meant. 'God Who Acts' was chosen to point up the contrast with the more customary expression, 'God Who Speaks'. Christian theology has tended to think of the Bible chiefly as 'the Word of God', though in point of fact a more accurate title would be 'the Acts of God'. The Word is certainly present in the Scripture, but it is rarely, if ever, dissociated from the Act; instead it is the accompaniment of the Act. To speak of the Bible solely as the Word, as has been done so frequently, incurs the risk of obscuring this fact with the result that the Word becomes a substantive, dissociated from history and dealt with as an abstraction. The sub-title, 'Biblical Theology as Recital', attempts to express the theme of the book in this light. The word 'recital' is not a particularly expressive term, but it was selected for want of a better one. At the centre of Biblical theology is a confession of faith of a particular type. It is not enough to say that Biblical theology is confessional by nature, because its distinguishing characteristic is to be determined chiefly by the question as to what type of confession is employed. The answer is clear that the Bible relates a certain history in a confessional manner, because the recounting of this history is the central religious act of the worshipping community. Hence it is here maintained that Biblical theology is *the confessional recital of the redemptive acts of God* in a particular history, because history is the chief medium of revelation. The term 'history' in this connection is used in a broad sense to include not only events of seeming impersonal significance, but also the lives of the individuals who compose it. The experience, the acts and the words of individuals are media of revelation, but individual personality and experience are not the centre of attention in and by themselves alone. They are the mediate means whereby God accomplishes his historical purposes, and the latter are more inclusive and comprehensive than the words, works and inner life of any one personality. The teachings of Jesus, for example, are for the Christian the revelation of the Word of God. Yet they do not form the centre of Christian theology in the sense that the expression, 'God's act in Christ', presents it, nor in the sense that it is stated in the classic creeds of the Church. This, then, is the point of view which the book defends and which the title attempts to express.

The writer is greatly indebted to his colleagues, Frank M. Cross, Jr., Floyd V. Filson and Joseph Haroutunian, on the faculty of McCormick Theological Seminary for their advice and counsel during the preparation of the manuscript. The last mentioned was particularly helpful in clarifying the writer's mind in regard to what he wished to say, in outlining the contents and in making suggestions concerning the problem of mythology. It was Dr. Cross, however, who laboured long and hard with the text itself, with the result that many improvements were made, though the many remaining weaknesses are not to be laid at his door. Professor H. H. Rowley and the Rev. Ronald Gregor Smith, in reading the manuscript for publication, have made a number of valuable suggestions to keep me from over-stating my thesis by inattention to other factors not emphasized. In the light of their comments certain additions and revisions have been made, though it may be that their advice has not been sufficiently followed for fear of weakening my central contentions. Gratitude must also be expressed to Professor Fred Denbeaux of Wellesley College for suggestions concerning the final chapter, in particular the definition of theology on pp. 108-9, and to President David L. Stitt, the faculty and the members of the Mid-Winter Convocation at the Austin Presbyterian Theological Seminary, February 5-9, 1951, for the opportunity to present this material and for their kindly hospitality, sympathetic interest and encouragement.

G. ERNEST WRIGHT

Chicago, Illinois
April 28, 1950

CHAPTER ONE

THE CHURCH'S NEED OF THE OLD TESTAMENT

I

MODERN theologians for some time have been writing about the radical transformation in the understanding of the gospel which came into being during the last century and which has had exceedingly serious consequences for the faith and mission of the Church. The one result of this transformation which here concerns us is the evident inability of large sections of the Church to take the Old Testament seriously as a primary revelation of God, of the nature of man and his institutions in human society, and of the Divine purpose in universal history. The scholarly study of the Old Testament has been separated from that of the New and from its mooring in the proclamation of the Church. By the end of the last century Christian scholars of the faith of Israel had become much more acclimated to the fields of general history, Oriental research and comparative religion than they were to the Church and to its traditional presuppositions. Thus while the Church still employed Old Testament scholars as teachers of the clergy, her heart was scarcely warmed by what they taught except in the heat of controversy with Fundamen talism. Consequently, by the time the first world war was over the occasional theological student who majored in the Old Testament was customarily on the defensive and the recipient of considerable derision from his fellow students in the practical departments and especially in the departments of the philosophy and psychology of religion. The serious study of the Old Testament was felt by the more virile minds of the Church to be an exercise of futility, the luxury of antiquarians who took no part in the vital concerns of the present time. Inevitably, therefore, the study of the Hebrew language increasingly came to be frowned upon by the great majority of the clergy as a foolish waste of time and money.

The result has been a rapid decline in both the quality and quantity of significant output on the part of the Church's Old Testament scholars. At the same time, it has meant, not only a rapid decline in the use of the Old Testament for the proclamation of the Gospel, but in many circles at least a radical distortion of that Gospel. Not long ago Godfrey E. Phillips presented the results of an inquiry which he had made regarding the use of the Old Testament in the mission field. Everywhere, especially among the intellectuals, he found uneasiness regarding it. The viewpoint of a pastor in north China is said to be representative of a very considerable section of opinion in that country:

> Intending missionaries or evangelists waste their time if they spend a lot of it studying the Old Testament. . . . The Old Testament teaching given in theological colleges in China is, in the experience of most students, devoid of interest or value for their after work. Reading the Old Testament is like eating a large crab; it turns out to be mostly shell, with very little meat in it. . . . We don't need to start with Moses and Elijah. It is enough to teach men about God as Jesus taught or revealed him.[1]

There is considerable evidence that a similar attitude exists in a large section of the Christian community in the West. Not that the Church would teach officially such a conception of its Scriptural treasury; yet it has been a drift of opinion. An evidence is the widely spread distribution of the New Testament and Psalms as the real Christian canon. Not by overt dogma but by actual practice, the Protestant Church has tended to emend radically the official canon of Scripture.

In other words, there has been a widespread revival of Marcionism in the modern Church, and many of the arguments against it employed by such Church Fathers as Tertullian need to be used again. There is a subtle difference, however, in that while Marcion rejected both paganism and the Old Testament with equal vigour, our modern rejection of paganism, except for the Communist type, is by no means as clear and forthright. To be sure, we inveigh against secularism, but we have not been clear as to where to draw the line between the Gospel and those forms of neo-paganism which are presented in terms of classical idealism. Perhaps, for example, we should not present Jesus

[1] *The Old Testament in the World Church* (London, 1942), p. 23.

Christ as One completely, radically and revolutionarily new, but as the fulfilment of the best idealism in existence among the heathen. Yet the question arises as to what kind of Christ is presented in such a situation. Surely, if the New Testament is not proclaimed as the fulfilment of the Old, if the Gospel as proclaimed by Jesus and by Paul is not the completion of the faith of Israel, then it must inevitably be a completion and fulfilment of something which we ourselves substitute—and that most certainly means a perversion of the Christian faith.

The new attitude toward the meaning of the Old Testament which came into being during the second half of the nineteenth century has been of tremendous value in the way it has encouraged the enthusiastic assemblage of a vast array of facts by means of which the Biblical literature must be understood. Unlike the liberal movement in New England of a century before, it encouraged Protestant scholarly study of the Bible to such an extent that the era between 1890 and 1910 may perhaps be designated as the greatest age of Biblical scholarship in Christian history, and no section of the World Church has remained untouched by the Protestant work which came to its culmination at that time. Yet because of certain difficulties inherent in its interpretative point of view, the great generation at the turn of the century was unable to reproduce itself. Old Testament scholarship, in England and America especially, has continued by and large along the lines then drawn, but it has done so with steadily diminishing returns.

Most important in the interpretative procedure of the last century was the conception of emergent value. In studying the Biblical materials the perception of the scholar was trained to look almost exclusively for a process of historical growth and development in which certain values emerge at each stage of the process. The earliest datable material was assumed to be the most 'primitive' and the later the more 'advanced'. Basic to one's understanding of the literature, therefore, was a certain scale of values by which the 'primitive' and the 'advanced' are to be so designated. This scale of values was and is usually implicit and unexamined. When forced to defend it, the scholar would attempt to explain it in some vague way as 'the mind of Christ'. Actually, however, it is more commonly seen today as a compound of conceptions derived from secular idealism, and not directly from the Bible. The Old Testament in such a viewpoint is important only in the sense that it provided the developmental background which lies *behind* the Gospel of Christ. It must be used by scholars for the historical understanding of the New Testament; but when the Gospel is formulated theologically or proclaimed by the Church to the world, one must deal only with the most 'advanced' stage of the revelation in which the values and ideals, so slow in emerging, appear in their purest form. If this be true, then the mission of the Church actually has no need of the Old Testament.

Yet today perhaps a majority of the Church's theological scholars have been placing large question marks before the assumptions of the 1900 era. Is the Bible primarily a textbook for values? Can its true significance be portrayed solely in emergent terms? Can the Divine self-disclosure by means of historical acts of grace and judgment be reduced to a philosophy of values? In other words, the proclamation (*kerygma*) of what God has done, whence it is inferred what he is, is the central concern of the Bible, apart from which a true understanding of the teaching (*didache*) is impossible. Yet this is precisely the point which the nineteenth century scholarship did not take seriously. When one conceives of the Bible as a textbook solely for *didache*, and then begins to examine other religions and to see numerous teachings which seem to have the same 'spiritual' and ethical interest, he begins to think of all religions as having a basic common denominator. The uniqueness and radical difference of Biblical faith is no longer comprehended, except as one attempts to argue that the teachings and 'values' of Christ are *superior* to those of the other religions in the sense that they are seen in him in a clearer and finer distillation. Thus the missionary has been tempted to present the 'superior' Christ and unwittingly to become an agent of the Western feeling of superiority in its patronizing dealing with the 'inferior' peoples. Thus the mission schools have been tempted merely to reproduce the idealism of Western liberal arts schools in the naive assumption that the teaching of values is the same as the proclamation of the Gospel. And thus also it has been

18

difficult for the Christian to draw a clear line of demarcation between the Biblical Gospel and pagan idealism.

II

One of the functions of the Old Testament in the Church has always been its role as a bulwark against paganism. That is to say, the Church has received an enlightenment from the faith of Israel which has enabled it to see that entrance into the Kingdom of Christ cannot be found among the religions of the world, but solely in the faith of Abraham and his seed, of which we are heirs in the Church by Jesus Christ. It is by the spectacles of the Old Testament that our eyes must be focussed upon the light in Christ; otherwise that light will be blurred and we shall not see it correctly. In support of these statements only a few observations can be made here.

Of basic importance for the Church is the realization that Israelite faith as represented in the earliest as well as in the latest literature was an utterly unique and radical departure from all contemporary pagan religions. The latter were all natural and cultural religions which had much more in common with one another than any one of them did with the Bible. There would appear to be certain tendencies in all pagan faiths which are normal constituents of the natural man's religion. Israel's breach of this 'normalcy' was something utterly new, phenomenal and radical. Consequently, the faith of Israel as fulfilled in Christ has always and will always bring to the Church such a sharpening of issues that the sword of the Gospel cannot be blunted completely among all Christians by compromise with pagan idealism.

Natural religion in Biblical times analyzed the problem of man over against nature. In the struggle for existence the function of religious worship was that of the integration of personal and social life with the natural world. Since man encounters in nature a plurality of uncontrollable powers to which he must adjust himself, he had isolated and identified these powers as the objects of his worship long before 3000 B.C. But in the ancient Near East, at least, polytheism was no primitive religion to be classified as merely one stage removed from animism and polydemonism, if the latter ever existed in pure textbook form. It was a highly sophisticated, organized and complex affair, in which the greatest intellectual achievement was the reduction of nature's vast plurality into an orderly and comprehensible system. The order of nature was believed to be an achievement in the integration of divine wills, in the pairing of complementary powers by means of the family and household patterns, and in the balancing of opposing forces such as life and death, rain and drought. The life of the individual was embedded in society and society was embedded in the rhythm and balance of nature which was the realm of the gods. The whole aim of existence was thus to fit into the rhythm and integration of the cosmic society of nature. While the law and order of human society was a function of one or more of the gods, sin was not primarily a violation of a gracious and righteous Divine will, a rebellion which destroyed personal communion, as in the Bible. It was rather more of an aberration which destroyed the harmony of affairs in the cosmic state. The good life was one which fitted into the established hierarchy of authority, beginning with the elder brother and the father in the family.

Polytheism was thus pre-eminently a religion of the *status quo*, and it is a significant fact that in no country where such religion has provided the cultural background has it ever been a dynamic force for social change. Allowed to develop long enough, the intellectuals may evolve from it a philosophical idealism, as in Plato, or a mysticism, as in Buddhism. Even here, however, the religion has not been a power for social evolution and social justice because of an inherent pessimism and the separation of the good life from the common life. In any case, the philosophical and mystical ways are for the few, while the common man has been left unredeemed from his superstitions.

In the faith of Israel, even in the earliest preserved literature, there is a radical and complete difference at every significant point. The Israelite did not analyze the problem of life over against nature. The latter plays a subordinate role in the faith, except as it is used by God to further his work in society and history. Instead, the problem of life is understood over against the will and purpose of the God who had chosen one people as the instrument of his universal, redemptive purpose (e.g. Gen. 12.3). This election of a people was not based upon merit, but upon a mysterious grace;

and its reality was confirmed by the great saving acts of this God, particularly as expressed in the redemption from Egyptian bond-age and in the gift of an inheritance. Here, then, is an utterly different God from the gods of all natural, cultural and philosophic religion. He is no immanent power in nature nor in the natural process of being and becoming. The nature of his being and will is revealed in his historical acts. He thus transcends nature, as he transcends history; and, consequently, he destroys the whole basis of pagan religion. No force or power *in* the world is more characteristic of him than any other, and it is increasingly under-stood today that the former identifications in early Israel of a Mountain-God, a Fertility-God and a War-God, from which the 'ethical monotheism' of the prophets gradually evolved, are fig-ments of scholarly presupposition and imagination. It is impos-sible on any empirical grounds to understand how the God of Israel could have evolved out of polytheism. He is unique, *sui generis*, utterly different.

One of the important doctrines of early as well as of late Israel, one which we have so zealously sought to set aside because it is so offensive to our good taste and to that of the naturalist and mystic of every age, is the doctrine of God's jealousy. This is an expression of the nature of God as he had revealed himself to Israel. It points directly to the utter difference between him and the gods, and it affirms that he alone is God, that he alone wills to be God, and that he will not put up with man's desire to worship tolerant powers of a lesser order, to whom he can integrate himself by a variety of processes, including magic, which he himself has evolved. The very nature of God's being places a tension at the heart of existence which destroys the natural man's integration of himself and his society in the rhythm of the kingdom of nature. The problem of life is not that of integration in the world. It is much deeper; it is the problem of obedience to the will of the transcendent Lord. He has bound his elect to himself, on the one hand, by great acts of love and grace, and, on the other hand, by a covenant in which his will is expressed. By means of these two elements of Biblical proclamation, the good news of salvation and the requirement of obedience, God wills to bind a people to himself by ties of love, faith and trust.

Sin is no longer aberration; it is a violation of communion, a betrayal of Divine love, a revolt against God's Lordship. It can be followed, therefore, only by humble repentance and Divine forgiveness. The pagan, on the contrary, may feel guilt, regret and despair at having fallen short of what was demanded of him, but he knows nothing of the Biblical sense of sin, contrition, repentance and forgiveness, of the joy that comes from doing God's will, or in any way of being undeserving of the Divine blessing heaped upon him.[1]

Biblical faith, therefore, could never be a religion of the *status quo* for its faithful adherents. Dynamic change and revolution are to be expected because God is a dynamic being, external to the processes of life, engaged in the active direction of history to his own goals. The tension which he places at the heart of existence excludes a peace of integration in the rhythmic cycle of nature. Human life must conform to his independent will, and his 'wrath' and 'judgment' are the Biblical means of expressing his active displeasure and his active work against all that flout his will.

Man's tendency toward, and desire for, pagan 'normalcy' being what they are, it is scarcely surprising to find that Christians have sought by a variety of means to avoid this conception and to eradicate the tension occasioned by the dynamic and energetic Lord who will even destroy in order to build. Many Israelites tried to avoid it by saying: 'It is not he; neither shall evil come upon us; neither shall we see sword nor famine' (Jer. 5.12). Men have always tried to escape from this God into deistic idolatry of one sort or another by saying that God does not see them and does not act directly in the affairs of earth. Greek philosophy and Eastern mysticism could certainly envisage no such deity, while in the ancient polytheisms the great gods were the aristocrats of the universe who for the most part were inaccessible to the common man and uninterested in him except as aristocrats are interested in the menial slaves who supply their needs.

The Christian idealist of this day has been very subtle in his rejection of this basic Biblical perception of the true nature of God. By setting the Old Testament to one side, he is not con-

---

[1] Cf. Henri Frankfort, *Kingship and the Gods* (Chicago, 1948), pp. 277 ff; *Ancient Egyptian Religion* (New York, 1948), pp. 73 ff.

fronted so directly with it and he can proceed to interpret the New Testament along more congenial lines. Among other things, he exhibits a distinct tendency to interpret God in 'spiritual' terms, and 'spiritual' entities are 'spiritually' discerned. The term 'spirit', derived from the conception of breath and wind, is of value when applied to God solely to prevent us from assuming that anthropomorphic language can exhaust the mystery and glory of his being. The difficulty with the term and with its derived adjective, 'spiritual', is that the human perception of God's being immediately becomes diffuse and without objective focus. The knowledge of God is reduced to a feeling, to an 'experience'. In the Protestant churches of our time no two words are in more common use than the terms 'spiritual' and 'experience'. And when the two are coupled together as 'spiritual experience', we have the popular conception of the sum total of religion, especially when the Golden Rule is added to it.

This represents the paganizing of the Gospel in a form that is pleasing to the cultured and sophisticated. It also presents the Gospel in a form that is more acceptable to the pagan idealist and to the Eastern scholar with mystical tendencies. This Gospel is no scandal nor stumbling block. Its tolerant diffuseness does away with the tension occasioned by the self-disclosure of the Biblical God. The reality of God's being becomes an immanent, inner experience which in practice, though not perhaps in theory, sets aside the whole Biblical doctrine of God's jealousy, the Biblical conception of the definite, dynamic, energetic Being whose transcendent holiness and objectivity are too great to be contained in 'experience', and as well the Biblical conception of the external, objective, historical acts of God. Is it not possible to suppose that God may not choose to reveal himself and his true nature primarily, if at all, in 'spiritual experience'? To be sure, there is an immediate awareness of God's presence in worship, in prayer, communion and confession; but the main emphasis of the Bible is certainly on his revelation of himself in historical acts, and in definite 'words', not in diffuse experience. There is an objectivity about Biblical faith which cannot be expressed in the language of inner experience. For this reason Biblical religion cannot be classified among the great mysticisms

23

of the world. It is scarcely an accident, therefore, that the Bible contains no *doctrine* of God's spirituality. It has a good deal to say about God's Spirit, or the Holy Spirit, but it does not employ metaphors derived from breath or wind as descriptive of his *essence* or *being*.[1] From beginning to end it uses the definite and concrete metaphors derived from human society, the most spectacular of all such anthropomorphs being the incarnation of Jesus Christ.

In other words, the Christian disuse of the Old Testament has left the Church an easy prey for the ubiquitous tendencies toward pagan 'normalcy' in which God's being or essence is conceived as in some way immanent in the processes of life, or, as in the more developed intellectual forms of paganism, as an ideal, a principle, a creative event, a vital urge, either within or without the evolving process. In every case, the tension created by God's Lordship, the radically serious conception of sin, and the reality of God's objective, historical acts of salvation are removed as the primary focus of the Christian's attention. In such a situation the distinction between the Church and the world of pagan idealism is difficult to maintain, and the Cross as the central symbol of the Church's faith no longer has the meaning it once had.

III

It has often been pointed out that the pagan religions have no sense of history. Polytheistic man, borne on the rhythmic cycle of nature, has no primary concern with history; instead his focus of attention is upon the yearly cycle in which life is recreated each spring and the blessing of order re-established. He is 'bound in the bundle of life' with nature, which is the kingdom of the gods, and his existence moves with the natural rhythm. Biblical man was 'bound in the bundle of life' with God who was not an immanence in nature but the Creator of nature, and who revealed

[1] Readers may wish to make an exception of the Johannine literature, basing the conclusion on John 4.24 ('God is spirit'). This statement must be interpreted, however, in the light of the whole Johannine vocabulary and in relation to the other Johannine sentences, 'God is light' and 'God is love'. When this is done, it is doubtful whether it can be used to sustain a *doctrine* of God's spirituality. These phrases are primarily concerned with the nature of the Divine *activity* and revelation, rather than with the ontology of God in the Hellenic sense.

24

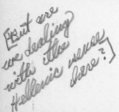
But are we dealing with this Hellenic sense here?

himself by means of historical acts in which there were also
historical promises. The focus of the Biblical man's attention,
therefore, was not on the cycle of nature, but on what God had
done, was doing and was yet to do according to his declared
intention. Promise and fulfilment thus become the central Biblical
themes, and the faithful man's attention was focussed on the
interpretation of his own life and of all history in this light. The
chief sources of his light and power came, not from individual or
isolated 'spiritual experiences', but from his certainty of the
reality of God's working in every event, from his concrete knowledge of God's power to save, to direct and to judge, from his
continued attempt to read the signs of the times in the light of
God's previous revelation, and from his glad acceptance of his
Divine election within the election of his people to do the work
God called him to do. His life and his work had meaning and
importance, therefore, because God fitted them into an over-
arching historical plan. God's revealed purpose was that the
whole earth shall become his kingdom, and the Israelite was
called to play his role in the universal cosmogony of the age yet
to be born. The faithful Israelite thus walked in time with a sure
and certain hope for the redemption of time. That hope burned
the more brilliantly in the desperate crises that meant the destruction of the hopes of paganism, for it was founded on the certainty
of God's historical promises; and God does not lie.

It is thus characteristic of Biblical faith that it creates this hope
that is based on trust. The pagan, on the other hand, has no such
resource. He does not know the God of history. He is uncon-
scious of any significant role he is called to play in history. He
knows of no personal election or of the election of his people,
except as selfish group desire is projected upon the gods. He is
an individualist who uses the elaborate means of worship solely
for the purpose of gaining his own security, integration and safety.
His vision is not lifted from himself to God's eternity. Consequently, in times of crisis when his security is removed, he is
uncertain where to turn. In Egypt he could only hope for a
beautiful, abundant hereafter; in Eastern religions for a better
reincarnation in which he was elevated above the evil and sorrow
of earth; in Canaanite and Mesopotamian religion there was little

to sustain him, for, when the individual's hope of earth was removed, there was no hope.

It is scarcely accidental, therefore, that the ancient polytheisms of the Biblical world died with the death of the civilizations of which they were the buttress. They had no means of interpreting history, and, when the gods could not provide order and security, they died. What survived from antiquity were such religions, on the one hand, as had no hope of earth but saw salvation as the individual attempt to climb the ladder of reason or mysticism out of earth's misery, and, on the other hand, Biblical faith with its firm insight in the redemption of God which is known most fully only in the very events which proved the downfall of the gods.

It is Israel which first broke radically with the pagan conceptions of the meaning of life and provided the view of history and the characteristic hope on which the New Testament and the Christian faith so firmly rest. If one leaves the Old Testament aside, he can still find these things present in the New Testament, but they are without historical focus and perspective. God's work in Christ is without meaning when separated from the time which is at hand and the kingdom now fulfilled (Mark 1.15). The Church which lacks the Old Testament again becomes easy prey to paganism and cannot provide the answer or the hope for the present desperate dilemma of man. Thus, on the one hand, the Church today has tended to succumb to man's hope for integration, happiness and security in the world as it is. It has preached the Gospel as a new kind of paganism, the value of which is strictly utilitarian. Religion is good for us; it gives us comfort and peace of mind; it is the only hope for democracy; it alone can support the *status quo* and make us happy within it. Yet Biblical hope and pagan comfort are not the same thing. In the present frustration within and without it is futile to speak glibly of peace when there is no peace. The Biblical hope is based solely upon God, upon his promises, and upon his election. It is known only in the context of judgment and of the Cross, in the acceptance of a severe ethical demand, of cross-bearing and cross-sharing and of a calling which one works out with fear and trembling. On the other hand, the Church has preached a Gospel of individual pietism and 'spiritual experience', separated almost completely

from the common life and from the historical programme of God
as revealed in the Bible, while emphasizing prayer and promising
the immortality of the soul. It is not that these things in themselves are totally wrong in their proper setting, but here they are
separated from their total Biblical context. As such, they are a
reversion to pagan 'normalcy', to an individualistic, self-centred,
utilitarian worship which lacks historical grounding in election,
promise and fulfilment. The question is critical as to whether
such faith can survive any better than did the ancient polytheisms.
Is it not a luxury solely of the prosperous?

One might ask, furthermore: What safeguards against paganizing tendencies have the Christian doctrines of man, of the
incarnation and the atonement, of the meaning and mission of
the Church, of the nature of the Kingdom of God, of the responsible or covenant society, if the Old Testament is separated from
the New and the latter left without the historical and theological
base on which it rests and which it has repaired and strengthened?
Certainly the Biblical concern with justice, while present in the
New Testament, is nevertheless centred in Israel's struggle for
the meaning of her national life in the covenant with God. In
the conception of worship it is Israel which first broke the completely new ground on which the Church now stands and from
which it receives nourishment. All pagan worship is based essentially on the conception of the efficacy of an individual's works,
whether of magic, sacrifice (food for the Deity's need), reason,
mystical exercise, or the giving of alms. In Israel, on the other
hand, proper worship begins with the proper inner attitude
toward God, with fear (holy reverence), faith, trust and love.
The sacrificial rites have lost their pagan setting and all thought
of God's physical need of food and drink is done away. Sacrifice
is instead a means which God provides whereby he may be worshipped, whereby sins may be atoned and communion re-established. It has no efficacy in the hands of the pagan or of the
hard-hearted sinner who commits his wickedness with premedi-
tation and a high hand. No atoning sacrifice will avail such a
person; he can only humble himself and with repentant heart
throw himself directly on the mercy of God. In other words, the
means of worship are efficacious only when properly used 'in

sincerity and truth' by faithful members of the covenant community (i.e. the Church), people whose lives exhibit integrity ('wholeness, perfection') in faithful obedience to God's will. The religious cultus which is used in any other way can provide no security in God; it is defiled and will suffer the fire of Divine judgment.

Furthermore, the central religious festivals are not rites of sympathetic magic, as in polytheism. In the latter, man takes on the form and identity of a god and acts out in a drama the role that God has played in the natural cycle. Thus by means of a process of identification man secures for himself the primal blessings and security of nature. But in Israel the major festivals of spring (Passover) and fall (the feast of the Tabernacles) had at their centre historical memory and commemoration in which the saving acts of God were rehearsed. Confessions of faith which were used in worship were nearly all recitals of what God had done. The first six books of the Old Testament have at their base precisely such a kerygmatic theme, one centring in the election of the fathers, the salvation at the Exodus, and the gift of a land in which to dwell. Around that theme the various editors have heaped a variety of material from numerous sources of tradition, but no Israelite was allowed to forget the simple history of God's acts which furnishes the underlying unity (e.g. Deut. 1-4; Josh. 24.1-13; Ps. 105; Acts 13.17-22).

This historical perspective of worship was carried over into the New Testament and into the Church. It is to be distinguished radically from pagan worship, and it cannot be maintained apart from the Old Testament. Biblical theology is first and foremost a theology of recital. The worshipper listens to the recital and by means of historical memory and identification he participates, so to speak, in the original events. Then facing his own situation he confesses his faith and his sin; he seeks God's forgiveness and direction; and he renews the vows of his covenant. In the modern Church, however, one wonders how much of the meaning of this conception of recital and of historical participation in the worship of God is actually retained. For what purpose is the Scripture read, Christian truth expounded, and the sacraments administered? There would appear to be a great uncertainty in the churches of our day about this question. The average Christian, however, seems to have little sense of the difference between Biblical and pagan worship, and like the pagan he is inclined to participate in the socially accepted religious cultus in search of security, without vigorous historical memory, without understanding of his sin, without forgiveness, and without renewal in a covenant community which has been founded by the redemptive activity of God.

It is not suggested here that the use of the Old Testament will automatically solve all of the problems facing the Christian Church! Yet it is suggested that the misuse and disuse of the Old Testament have deprived the Church of its Bible. The New Testament is not itself a Bible; it is a small body of literature filled with all sorts of presuppositions which have no meaning to the uninitiated. It is the Old Testament which initially broke radically with pagan religion and which thus forms the basis on which the New rests. Christ came in the fulness of time, not time in general, but God's special time which began with Abraham. To be sure, the Old Testament by itself does not present a faith by which men today can live. Judaism and Christianity are two different religions because in the former the Old Testament is made relevant, is seen fulfilled in the Talmud, while in the latter it is fulfilled in Christ. For the Christian, Christ is the key to the central contents of the Old Testament, but at the same time it is the Old Testament which provides the clue to Christ. It is small wonder, then, that when a Christian seriously seeks to explain and expound his faith over against another religion, his initial and basic arguments are drawn from the Old Testament, for it is the latter which has been a chief bulwark of the Church against paganism.[1]

IV

If this be true, then one of the most important tasks of the Church today is to lay hold upon a Biblically centred theology. To do so means that we must first take the faith of Israel seriously and by the use of the scholarly tools at our disposal seek to

[1] For fuller discussion, with supporting detail and references, of the arguments here presented for the distinction between Israelite faith and that of polytheism, see the writer's monograph, *The Old Testament Against Its Environment* (London and Chicago, 1950).

understand the theology of the Old Testament. But, secondly, as Christians we must also press toward a *Biblical* theology, in which both Testaments are held together in an organic manner. We cannot envisage the task ahead as merely that of studying New Testament theology and Old Testament theology in separate compartments, and then attempting to put them together. It is very doubtful whether one can maintain a New Testament theology as a separate and independent discipline. The New Testament is primarily that fulfilment of the Old Testament which separates the faith from its nationalistic basis and with Christ as the king of the new Israel it unifies that which is not unified in old Israel. It restores the power of the earlier eschatology, and in the cross and resurrection brings together God's justice and love, his wrath and his salvation, his gospel and his law, so that the Church is sent into the world conscious both of the long history of God's activity behind it and of its new creation in Jesus Christ. The New Testament in and by itself alone is an insufficient base on which to stand. The significance of God's work in Jesus Christ can be comprehended only when the Bible is retained *as the Bible*, not as an abbreviated torso of the Bible.

Yet how are we to proceed in such a task? Biblical scholars divide themselves into Old Testament specialists and New Testament specialists, and our theological seminaries have Old Testament and New Testament departments. An occasional seminary in America still attempts to bridge the gap by something called the Department of English Bible, as though the only prerequisite for Biblical understanding were a knowledge of the English language, while those who are able to teach the Biblical languages are by their knowledge incapacitated for the communication of Biblical truth in the language of their nativity.

Even more important is the fact that Biblical scholars today are very uncertain as to how to move in the direction of Biblical theology. The point of view of the last century resulted in numerous histories of Israelite religion, but in very little theology. We now see the inadequacy of the former approach, but how are we to proceed in our attempt to do something different? The focus of attention formerly was concentrated on the analysis of history and literary forms, with the result that the Bible was split into its many component parts with little to hold them together except the conception of an evolving historical process. An extreme example of this type of work was published recently, as though born long after its time: I. G. Matthews, *The Religious Pilgrimage of Israel* (New York and London, 1947). This author presents Israel's history as evolving through some fourteen different religions or distinct religious formulations. The final chapter on the religion of Judaism (400 B.C.–A.D. 135) scarcely mentions the early Christian movement, except for one brief paragraph on the Nazarenes, thus emphasizing the complete separation of the Old and New Testaments. In such a viewpoint a Biblical theology is completely impossible because the Bible has no unity; it speaks by means of many human voices which present more dissonance than they do harmonious concord of sound.[1]

Fortunately, most Biblical scholars today are unwilling to surrender to such a view. After all, the Bible does testify to a certain religious faith which, like other faiths, is a distinct entity of which its adherents were very self-conscious. The process of history brought changes and developments within the faith, but not of such a nature as to shift it completely to a different religion. To deny this seems a violation of the whole procedure of scholarly research and an exhibition of a serious myopia which renders one incapable of seeing the forest for the trees. Thus most scholars today who are seriously interested in Biblical theology believe that it is possible and necessary to deal with Biblical religion as an historical reality in its structural unity, and not alone in its chronological development.

Yet the problem is still acute as to how the historical and the systematic approaches are to be combined. Indeed, there is a real question as to whether Biblical faith can be compressed into a 'system' at all. On the one hand, it is filled with paradox so that one no sooner makes one type of statement on the basis of one selection of verses than he may be confronted with other passages which seem to say the opposite. The world is good; but it is also

---

[1] See further in more detail Robert C. Dentan, *Preface to Old Testament Theology* (New Haven, 1950), Chaps. V-VII; and James D. Smart, 'The Death and Rebirth of Old Testament Theology', *Journal of Religion*, Vol. XXIII (1943), pp. 1-11, 125-136.

evil. Man is a free lord of this world; yet he is not free because God is Lord. God loves man above all creatures, but turns on him with a terrible wrath. God chooses Israel and sets his love on her; yet his election brings with it a continuous suffering. Many of the Biblical paradoxes can be resolved by rational statement to be sure, but, taken as a whole, Biblical faith can no more be confined to a rigorous system than can life itself.

On the other hand, the Biblical language is concrete, poetical, metaphorical, picturesque. Nearly all of its religious vocabulary is derived from sources in human life which immediately bring pictures or images to the mind and which are filled with colour, contrast and movement. Consequently, the Biblical language will always be the despair of the precise and exact theologian who above all desires a simple, coherent system. When one tries to translate this language out of the paradoxical colour and movement of life into abstract, universal concepts and propositions, he immediately finds that the vitality of the faith has eluded him. Must we assume, therefore, that to theologize from the Biblical language means that we are immediately separating ourselves from the faith? The answer is certainly in the affirmative, if to theologize means first and foremost the reduction of the colourful image into a dreary black and white so that a consistent system may be erected with a minimum of paradox. Yet man cannot live by consistency or by the abstract, colourless, universal truth. One must ask, therefore, whether our concern with the abstract and with the systematic should occupy the centre of our attention as we approach the subject matter of Biblical theology. Is it possible that there may be another kind of theology than the abstract, the coherent and the propositional? I believe that there is, and that Biblical theology is more to be characterized by the words 'confessional recital' than it is by 'a system of ideas'. It is a reflection on the meaning of God's acts more than it is 'a study of the religious ideas of the Bible in their historic context'.[1] If this is the case, then perhaps a number of our initial difficulties with the subject may be removed.

---

[1] Contrast Dentan, *op. cit.*, p. 45.

CHAPTER TWO

THEOLOGY AS RECITAL

I

BIBLICAL theology has long been dominated by the interests of dogmatic or systematic theology. Indeed, throughout the first three centuries of Protestantism the two disciplines were scarcely distinguished, at least among conservative churchmen. All theology was Biblical theology in the sense that it was a system of doctrine drawn from the Bible and supported by collections of proof-texts. While the fact of the Reformation is illustrative of the perennial tension which has always existed between the Bible and theology, nevertheless the separation of Biblical theology as an independent subject of study occurred in a new form within pietism and eighteenth century rationalism, when the Bible was used to criticize orthodox dogma. Johann Philipp Gabler in 1787 seems to have been the first in modern times formally to advocate a distinction between the two disciplines. To him Biblical theology is an objective, historical discipline which attempts to describe what the Biblical writers thought about divine matters. Dogmatic theology, on the other hand, is didactic in character and sets forth what a theologian philosophically and rationally decides about divine matters in accordance with his time and situation.[1] Nevertheless, in organizing the data of Biblical faith the rubrics of systematic theology continued in use, the chief of these being the doctrine of God, the doctrine of man, and the doctrine of salvation.

During the nineteenth century, however, the historical nature of the Bible was more clearly seen than ever before. As a result, men came to believe that Biblical theology must concern itself primarily with the development of religious ideas. This point of view made the task of the Biblical theologian so difficult that few scholars attempted anything other than a history of religion in the Old and New Testaments. Perhaps the greatest work in Old Testament theology produced during the last century was

---

[1] So Robert C. Dentan, *Preface to Old Testament Theology* (New Haven, 1950), p. 8.

that by the German scholar Hermann Schultz.[1] He tried to solve the problem by presenting first a historical account of the development of Israel's religion and then by giving a topical treatment in which theological concepts were traced through the various historical periods. In other words, no attempt was made to present a systematic theology of the Old Testament as a whole. The growth of religious concepts through the history was thought to be too great to permit a systematic survey. A different type of treatment is illustrated by the work of the French pastor, Ch. Piepenbring, first published in 1886.[2] He presented three cross sections through Israel's history, the first being the pre-prophetic period beginning with Moses, the second the age of prophecy, and the third the Exilic and post-Exilic age. In each period he systematically treated the doctrines of God, man, worship and salvation under a variety of chapter headings.

It will be noted that these works are based upon two presuppositions. The first is that the evolution of religious concepts in the Bible is so great that there are virtually different theologies in different periods. The second is that the procedure of dogmatic theology is normative for all theology, including that of the Bible. If both these presuppositions are correct, then the task of Biblical theology is quite clear. It is either to trace the evolving history of religious concepts through the various Biblical periods, as did Schultz, or else it is to take a cross section through the Bible at one period and treat that as systematically as possible.

With regard to the first presupposition there is an increasingly widespread belief today that while historical development is indeed a very important factor in the Bible yet it is one which has been overemphasized. A living organism is not a blank tablet on which all writing is done by environmental, geographical and historical conditioning. If it were, then a description of a historical process might be sufficient to enable us to comprehend its inner significance. But in every organism there is something given which determines what it is and what it will become. Environment and geography can explain many things in ancient

[1] See his *Old Testament Theology* (translated from the 4th German ed. by J. A Paterson, in 2 vols., Edinburgh, 1892).

[2] *Theology of the Old Testament* (translated from the French by H. G. Mitchell Boston, 1893).

Israel, but they cannot explain why Israel did not undergo the same type of evolution as did her pagan neighbours, nor why the early Church did not become another Jewish purist sect or Hellenistic mystery religion. One explanation for this difference in evolution which positivist scholars have been wont to give is the presence in Biblical history of a remarkable series of religious geniuses: Moses, the prophets, Jesus, Paul. Yet every genius is in part a product of his historical situation in a given social context. He cannot be explained apart from certain inner, spiritual factors which are a vital part of the cultural situation in which he arose. In other words, there is in the Bible something far more basic than the conceptions of environment, growth and genius are able to depict. It is this 'given' which provided the Bible's basic unity in the midst of its variety and which sets Biblical faith apart as something radically different from all other faiths of mankind.[1]

The realization of this fact leads most Biblical scholars today to believe that far more unity exists in the Bible than was conceived fifty years ago. They are thus confident that a Biblical theology is possible which is something other than the history of the Bible's religious evolution. Yet, for the most part, the second presupposition mentioned above is still accepted. That is to the effect that theology is propositional dogmatics, the systematic presentation of abstract propositions or beliefs about God, man and salvation. The churches retain and encourage this conception in their liturgy and creeds. For example, every elder, deacon, commissioned church worker and minister in the Presbyterian Church of the U.S.A. is required to affirm when he or she is ordained that the confession of faith of that church contains 'the system of doctrine taught in the Holy Scriptures'. But does the Bible contain a *system* of doctrine? Certainly none of its writers was primarily concerned with the presentation of such a scheme. Consequently, we must say that static, propositional systems are those which the Church itself erects by inference from the Biblical writings. The systems are very good and very important, but we

[1] See further the monograph by the writer, *The Old Testament Against its Environment*, and that by Floyd V. Filson, *The New Testament Against its Environment* (London and Chicago, 1950).

cannot define the Bible by means of them. No system of propositions can deal adequately with the inner dynamics of Biblical
faith.

Yet most of the recent attempts to describe the theology of the
Old and New Testaments proceed along the old lines by adopting
the rubrics of dogmatic theology and by attempting to force
Biblical faith into this mould.[1] Indeed, one of the most serious
and careful discussions of the history and nature of Old Testament
theology, that of Robert C. Dentan published in 1950, concludes
that the discipline is to be defined as 'that Christian theological
discipline which treats of the religious ideas of the Old Testament
systematically, i.e. not from the point of view of the historical
development, but from that of the structural unity of Old Testament religion, and which gives due regard to the historical and
ideological relationship of that religion to the religion of the New
Testament'.[2] Since any arrangement of the material will be one
which we impose from the outside, he believes it best to adopt
one which is simple and meaningful to us. 'For this purpose it
seems difficult to think of a better outline than that which is used

[1] Thus, for example, Ludwig Köhler, *Theologie des Alten Testaments* (Zweite
Auflage, Tübingen, 1947), attempts to organize the data under the basic headings
of God, man and salvation. So also with elaboration does Paul Heinisch, *Theology
of the Old Testament* (tr. from the German by Rev. Wm. Heidt, Collegeville, Minn.,
1950). Otto J. Baab, *Theology of the Old Testament* (New York and Nashville, 1949),
follows the same pattern with the insertion of chapters on sin, the Kingdom, death
and evil. Millar Burrows, *An Outline of Biblical Theology* (Philadelphia, 1946), is a
very useful, descriptive work which attempts to treat the whole Bible together.
Introductory considerations on authority and revelation are followed by three
chapters on the conceptions of God, Christ and the universe. These are followed
by Chaps. VI-IX which deal with anthropology, Chaps. X-XII with soteriology,
and Chaps. XIII-XVIII with the worship and service of God. Perhaps the greatest
work on Old Testament theology ever produced is the three volume treatment of
Walther Eichrodt, *Theologie des Alten Testaments* (Leipzig, 1933-39). He attempts to
organize the material under three headings, God and People, God and the World,
God and Man. This arrangement has been criticized because it leads to repetition
and overlapping. The chief unifying element he takes to be the covenant. This too
has been criticized as a serious weakness since it has been commonly held that the 'idea
of the Covenant is far from omnipresent in the Old Testament and only by a *tour de
force* can it be made to appear so' (so Dentan, *op. cit.*, p. 38). This writer can only
agree with the criticism in part, and for a different reason. That is that election is
more primary in Israel than covenant. While the two go together, the latter is a
conceptual language for expressing the meaning of the former and it makes considerable difference as to which receives the primary emphasis. Yet, whatever we
may say, Eichrodt has seen more clearly than anyone else the danger of using the
categories of dogmatic theology for Biblical theology. His work is an extremely
significant pioneer effort which attempts to hew a new path.

[2] *Op. cit.*, pp. 48 and 66.

36

by systematic theology, since this outline arose from an attempt to answer the basic questions concerning human life: What is the nature of God in His perfection? (theology); what is the nature of man in his weakness? (anthropology); what is the nature of that dynamic process by which man's weakness becomes reconciled with God's perfection? (soteriology).'[1]

Simple and persuasive though this point of view appears to be, it fails to take into account the fact that the Biblical writers were uninterested in ideas in the sense that we are. They were not primarily systematic teachers of religious ideas. Are we to assume, then, that Biblical theology is solely a modern discipline which we seek to impose on a literature that is devoid of any *primary* interest in it? I should rather say that we must first ascertain the central interest and methodology of the Biblical writers and define Biblical theology accordingly. Otherwise, how can it be the serious, historical discipline that we insist it must be? The rubrics of systematic theology are too abstract and universalized to fit the Biblical point of view. The exclusive use of them must of necessity compel us to do violence to that standpoint, to omit large sections of material or at least to arrange them in such a way that their proper interrelation is obscured. Can another way be found which is more in keeping with the Biblical material itself? Unless there is, then we should abandon the whole conception of Biblical theology to those who insist that it must be nothing more than the popularization and preaching of the faith to the modern day.[2]

Such is our present dilemma. Is Biblical theology a history of Biblical ideas? Is it a systematic cross-section of those ideas, treated under the rubrics of a dogmatic theology which the Bible does not possess? Or is it merely the packaging of the foods of

[1] *Ibid.*, p. 64.
[2] Cf., for example, Millar Burrows, *Journal of Bible and Religion*, Vol. XIV, No. 1 (Feb. 1946), p. 13: 'The task of biblical theology is, as I see it, to bridge the yawning chasm between our basic critical studies ... and the practical use of the Bible in preaching and religious education ... Biblical theology must package the foods for the consumer.' Cf. also, Otto Eissfeldt, *Zeitschrift für die alttestamentliche Wissenschaft*, Vol. XLIV (1926), pp. 1-12, who sees the distinction between the history of Biblical religion and Biblical theology as the distinction between the methods of reason and faith. The latter takes seriously only those elements which are regarded as the revelation of God in the Bible by the particular point of view, confession or church to which one adheres.

Biblical research for the consumer in the Christian Church? Most of our current thinking seems to be wavering among these three procedures.

II

In considering Biblical faith, it seems to me that the point at which we must begin is not with the history of its evolving ideas but with history in another sense. It is history as the arena of God's activity. Biblical theology is first and foremost a theology of recital, in which Biblical man confesses his faith by reciting the formative events of his history as the redemptive handiwork of God. The realism of the Bible consists in its close attention to the facts of history and of tradition because these facts are the facts of God.

A comparison of the Bible with the religious literatures of other people points up this fact as its chief distinguishing characteristic. Why is the Bible in contradistinction to all other 'bibles' centred in the story of the life and historical traditions of one people? To ask this question is virtually to ask why the Bible is what it is. The national literature of other people of the time exhibits no such interest in history. To be sure, the ancient kings and nobles of Egypt, Canaan and Mesopotamia had many historical inscriptions and records inscribed on stelae, and on temple, tomb and palace walls. Such annals, however, were concerned almost solely with the personal glorification of those for whom they were prepared. The Egyptians produced a number of excellent short stories, while the Babylonians composed the remarkable Babylonian Chronicle. Yet these are scarcely serious attempts to write history, even though historical events are recorded; they had another purpose altogether. The specifically religious literature of the ancient polytheist contained numerous tales of demi-gods and heroes, but actually it was not interested at all in history as such since the primary focus of its attention was upon nature. A great deal has been written to compare the literature of Israel with that of its environment, but one will note that the only worthwhile comparisons are in the areas of law, poetry, didactic or proverbial sayings and creation myths. In aesthetic, imaginative and affective faculties Israelite literature, it is affirmed, is by no means inferior

38

to the products of the great civilizations of the ancient Near East; indeed in most respects it is superior to them. In fact, says Professor W. F. Albright, 'a very large section of modern religion, literature and art actually represents a pronounced retrogression when compared with the Old Testament'.[1] Yet when all has been said about the comparison of the literature of Israel with the other literatures of the Near East, the most obvious difference is the one most rarely touched upon: that is the peculiar Israelite attention to historical traditions. The Biblical point of view is concentrated, not merely on the individual exploits of heroes and kings, not merely on court annals like the Babylonian Chronicle which were especially important for the calendar and the royal archives, but rather on the unity and meaningfulness of universal history from the beginning of time until the end of time. It is in the framework of this universal history that the chronicles of individual events are set and ultimately receive their meaning.

It was impossible for the ancient polytheist to have a primary interest in history as such, because, as was pointed out in Chapter One, the concentration of his attention was upon *nature*, not history. Nature was the indigenous realm of the superhuman, and the forces of nature were the gods he worshipped. Man experienced in nature a plurality of these powers. Yet world order had been established through a delicate process of integration of divine wills and through the establishment of a hierarchy of authority. Man's security was found in the way he fitted himself into this divine harmony. His religious literature was inevitably centred in nature myths which depicted the action and interaction of the powers that produced this harmony. Man's greatest good was to be caught up within this cosmic rhythm of nature. Consequently his life moved in a cycle corresponding to the cycle of nature. The miracle of renewal and birth in the spring, followed by the decline and death of summer, by revival in the fall and again by the miracle of spring—such was the movement of nature. Such also was the movement of human life, for man was born along with the rise and fall of nature's life. This rhythmic move-

---

[1] *Archaeology and the Religion of Israel* (Baltimore, 1942), p. 33. Chapter I of this book is a fresh treatment of this whole question. Cf. further T. Eric Peet, *A Comparative Study of the Literatures of Egypt, Palestine, and Mesopotamia* (London, 1931).

ment was the greatest good which natural religion had to bestow upon human existence. Consequently, such religion could never have any real concern with history, unless one is to define history as this rhythmic natural cycle, repeated anew each year. The religious literature of the polytheist, therefore, was concerned with the mythological stories of the gods, together with the great variety of hymns, prayers, incantations, sacrificial regulations and the like, by means of which the natural powers were worshipped.

In India, China and Persia religion developed from this polytheistic base into higher and more sophisticated forms. Indeed, in Persia especially Zoroastrianism represents, at least in its original form, a radical departure from typical polytheism. Yet the type of religious literature produced in all those countries is very different from the Bible. The Veda of Hinduism, the Pali literature of Buddhism, the Confucian Classics, and the Avesta of Zoroastrianism are all composed for the most part of liturgical material and especially of *teachings* on a great variety of subjects. None of them has any particular historical interest. Even the Koran of Islam, a religious heresy of Biblical faith, is chiefly a series of teachings from the auditions and visions of the prophet Mohammed. There are numerous stories in all this literature, but the interest is not as a rule in the story but in the teaching which it is meant to convey.

In Greece, on the other hand, there was indeed an interest in history and in historical traditions. It is with Herodotus and Thucydides of the fifth century B.C. that the modern historian of history first feels himself at home.[1] The achievements of these men and of those who preceded and followed them, are indeed amazing in that ancient world, for it was the Greeks who liberated the mind from shackles of what has been called the mythopoeic apprehension of reality which characterizes polytheism.[2] Yet they never achieved that view of human history as a meaningful process *en route* to a goal which is the chief characteristic of Biblical writers. History was not primarily a theological pro-

[1] Cf. James T. Shotwell, *The History of History* (New York, 1939), Vol. I, Part III; James W. Thomson and Bernard J. Holm, *A History of Historical Writing* (New York, 1942), Vol. I, Chap. II.
[2] Cf. H. and H. A. Frankfort in *The Intellectual Adventure of Ancient Man* (Chicago, 1946), pp. 373 ff.

duction with a theological purpose. This is true of the philosophers as well as of the historians. History remained for them all a cyclical process. The circle of events was never broken and straightened out into a line. One writer has said about Aristotle, for example, that he

> appears to leave no place for historical development in the animated kingdom. He admits, indeed, that the human race has at different times and in different places grown out of barbarism into civilization, and by the progressive cultivation of art, science, and philosophy had repeatedly attained perfection. Whenever this had taken place, he thinks that deluges or other convulsions of nature must have swept away the entire race, all but a few individuals left on the mountain tops, or otherwise preserved for the repopulation of the earth, left, however, as under such circumstances would necessarily have been the case, destitute of all the apparatus of the arts, and having to begin again *de novo* the development of civilization. With this strange conception of a cyclical rise and fall in the civil history of mankind, Aristotle combined the view that Nature as a whole is eternal, and must for ever have been in all essential particulars just as it is now.[1]

For Herodotus the war between the Greeks and Persians was an inevitable conflict of opposites. The equilibrium of the world had been destroyed by the accumulation of vast human and material resources in the hands of the Persian king. The nemesis which overwhelmed Xerxes restored the harmony or equilibrium of affairs. History is thus like the oscillation of a pendulum; matter or substance in this world is in continuous motion, the elements of which ceaselessly group and regroup themselves in a monotonous upward and downward curve. Such a view excludes completely any prospect of progress or movement toward an earthly millennium, whether the latter is to be achieved through the gradual evolution envisaged by modern liberal idealism, or through the revolution conceived by Marxist communism. History is in movement, but it is going nowhere. It is filled with

[1] Quoted from a review of Grote's *Aristotle*, which appeared in 1872, by Thompson and Holm, *op. cit.*, p. 37.

41

forces which move on an upward or downward path or else in a circle as though around a wheel. Consequently, when Christianity entered the classical world, it encountered great difficulty in making itself understood over against the pagan conception of history. Origen, for example, in protesting against the theory of cycles derides the idea that in another Athens sometime in the future there will be another Socrates married to another Xanthippe. And Augustine cannot conceive of another Plato teaching his pupils in another Academy in a succession of ages endlessly repeated. 'God forbid', he says, 'that we should swallow such nonsense! Christ died, once and for all, for our sins.' Human history, on the contrary, far from consisting of a series of repetitive patterns, is in sure movement, even though unsteady, to an ultimate goal.[1]

Israel broke with the ancient conceptions in the first instance because of a radically different view of God. As the philosopher Hegel pointed out over a century ago, when we enter the Old Testament we find that: 'Nature—which in the East is the primary and fundamental existence—is now depressed to the condition of a mere creature . . . God is known as the creator of all men, as he is of all nature, and as absolute causality generally.' It is true, he observes, that in India there existed 'the pure conception of "Brahm"; but only as the universal being of Nature; and with this limitation, that Brahm is not himself an object of consciousness. Among the Persians we saw this abstract being become an object of consciousness, but it was that of sensuous intuition—as Light. But the idea of Light has at this stage [in Judaea] advanced to that of "Jehovah"—the *purely One*.'[2]

Biblical man conceived of himself as existing in a particular, unique history which possessed significance because God through it was revealed as in process of redeeming all history. Thus while the Israelite existed in nature, he was lord of nature, using and subduing it for his own purposes, and his focus of attention was

[1] See C. N. Cochrane, *Christianity and Classical Culture* (London, New York and Toronto, 1944), pp. 245, 467 f, 483 f. Cf. also the brief treatment in Oscar Cullmann, *Christ and Time* (Tr. from the German by Floyd V. Filson; Philadelphia, 1950, London, 1951), pp. 51-60.

[2] Georg Wilhelm Friedrich Hegel, *The Philosophy of History* (tr. by J. Sibree; revised ed., New York, 1900), p. 195.

not on nature but on history. Nature was not an independent object nor the kingdom of powers to be worshipped; it was instead a handmaiden, a servant of history.

How had Israel, in the first instance, arrived at such a view? It was certainly not because there existed in the nation a series of great metaphysical philosophers. On the contrary, the religious leaders were uninterested in anything which might be considered abstract philosophy. We can never be certain of the true reason for this particular Israelite view of nature and history. It is the one primary, irreducible datum of Biblical theology, without antecedents in the environment whence it might have evolved. The earliest forms of literature which Israel produced are filled with it. This is evidently true, not only of the oldest preserved poetry and prose, but of works which are quoted though not preserved: e.g. 'the Book of the Wars of Yahweh' (Num. 21.14) and 'The Book of Yashar (or, of the Upright)' (Josh. 10.13; II Sam. 1.18). It is likewise true of the traditions as they were circulated in their pre-literary forms.

The most probable supposition regarding the origin of Israel's preoccupation with history is that it arose in the earliest days of the nation's history as the only possible explanation available to the people of the manner in which God had made himself known to them. As Walter Eichrodt has written:

> The roots of this peculiar viewpoint, by which Israel clearly is to be differentiated from all other Near Eastern peoples, doubtless lie in those happenings of the early time, which gave the impulse to the genesis of the Israelite people, in the events of the time of Moses. The deliverance from Egypt and the uniting of kin and families of wandering cattle-breeders in a sacral tribal covenant during the wilderness period were those [events] which have impressed the national Israelite consciousness as the basis and determining acts for all time of the Divine self-disclosure. If one observes the completely unique importance which these events have gained in the total religious praxis and tradition, in the cultic hymns no less than in the prophetic admonitions, in the liturgy and cultic instruction of the priests as well as in the parental teaching to the children, in the explanation of the pastoral and agricultural festivals no less

43

than in the establishment of all law-giving at the time of Moses, then no doubt can exist that this first experience of a Divine encounter was decisive for the fundamental conception of the Divine revelation in Israel. Here one learned to understand the being of God from history and to exhibit his works in the forms of history.[1]

At the centre of Israelite faith lay the great proclamation that the God of the fathers had heard the cry of a weak, oppressed people in Egypt. They had been slaves, but then freed by mighty acts which demonstrated God's power to the Egyptians and to the world. As slaves for whom the justice of the world made no provision, they were delivered by a most extraordinary exhibition of Divine grace. This was a sign, a wonder, not to be explained by fortune or irrational chance, but solely by the assumption of a personal Power greater than all the powers of this world. This was a God who could make the forces of nature serve him as well as the recalcitrance of the heart of Pharaoh. He was one who for some reason had set his love on a defenceless people and had chosen them for his own.

Israel's doctrine of God, therefore, was not derived from systematic or speculative thought, but rather in the first instance from the attempt to explain the events which led to the establishment of the nation. While living in the world of natural religion, they focussed their attention, not on nature and the gods of nature, but on the God who had revealed himself in an extraordinary series of historical events. The knowledge of God was an inference from what actually had happened in human history. The Israelite eye was thus trained to take human events seriously, because in them was to be learned more clearly than anywhere else what God willed and what he was about. Consequently, in all that happened subsequently the Israelite simply interpreted the meaning of events by recognizing and acknowledging in them the God who had formed the nation by the remarkable events at the Exodus and in the wilderness. The half-hearted, fearful and defeated attempt to break into Canaan from Kadesh-barnea in

[1] Walther Eichrodt, 'Offenbarung und Geschichte im Alten Testament', *Theologische Zeitschrift*, 4. Jahrgang, Heft 5 (Sept./Okt., 1948), p. 322. Cf. also Artur Weiser, *Glaube und Geschichte im Alten Testament* (Stuttgart, 1931), pp. 4 ff.

the south was attributed to rebellion against God and lack of faith in his leadership (Num. 14; Deut. 2.26-46). The long stay in the wilderness thus was seen to be God's judgment upon the people for their sin. Yet subsequently the successes of the conquest of Canaan were occasioned solely by the powerful leadership of Yahweh. The initial defeat at Ai in the tradition found ready explanation in Achan's violation of the Divine command that all booty was to be 'devoted' to God and none was to be taken for personal gain. The ideology of Holy War depicted in the books of Deuteronomy, Joshua and Judges was more than a mere rationalization for the nation's wars. It was based on the recognition that God who had saved Israel at the Exodus had a historical purpose and programme. The battles of Joshua and the Judges, therefore, were more than the mere fightings of men; they were holy because they were God's war. According to an old fragment of the law of this Holy War, a priest was required to explain to the army whenever it was ready to go into battle: 'Hear, O Israel, ye approach this day unto battle against your enemies. Let not your hearts faint; fear not, and do not tremble, neither be ye terrified because of them; for Yahweh your God is he that goeth with you, to fight for you against your enemies, to save you' (Deut. 20.3-4).[1]

When Israel settled in Canaan and attempted to make their living from the soil, it was easy for many of them simply to interpret the agricultural pursuits in the same manner as their Canaanite neighbours and teachers. Thus, we are told, they 'did evil in the sight of Yahweh, and served Baalim. And they forsook Yahweh, God of their fathers, who brought them out of the land of Egypt, and followed other gods, of the gods of the people that were round about them, and bowed themselves unto them, and provoked Yahweh to anger' (Judg. 2.11-12). It was thus possible to interpret the wars of the period of the Judges in this light. The judgment and the grace of God were seen in the oppressions and deliverances, and correlated with the idolatry, repentance and faith of the people.

When Israel was caught up within the struggles of the world

---

[1] See further Gerhard von Rad, *Deuteronomium-Studien* (Göttingen, 1947), pp. 30-41; and *Der Heilige Kreig im alten Israel* (Zürich; 1951).

powers during the first great empire-building epoch of history, Yahweh was not lost within the events nor did he perish with the state he had founded. On the contrary, he rescued a remnant as a brand from the burning. For with what must have seemed to pagans as infinite presumption Israel proclaimed that it was Yahweh himself who was directing these wars to his own ends, even though the conquering armies did not know or acknowledge it. The Assyrian was the 'rod of his anger' (Isa. 10.5); Nebuchadnezzar was his 'servant' (Jer. 29.5); and Cyrus was his 'anointed' (Isa. 45.1). Let all the nations be gathered together, said Second Isaiah; let them take counsel and see if they can interpret either past or present (Isa. 43.8-9). Let them haste in the confusion of preparing their idols. Let these gods 'bring forth and show us what shall happen; let them show the former things, what they are, that we may consider them and know the latter end of them, or declare us things to come. Show us the things that are to come hereafter, that we may know that ye are gods. . . . Behold, ye are as nothing, and your work is of nought. An abomination is he that chooseth you' (Isa. 41.7, 21-24).[1] Yahweh alone is in charge of history. As one who had met Israel in historical event, he thus was recognised as the Lord of all events who was directing the whole course of history to his own ends, for nothing happened in which his power was not acknowledged.

III

This meant that nature could not be left to the prerogatives of the pagan Baal. The epithets and functions of this Canaanite god of the storm were taken over for Yahweh. Lightning was his arrow and thunder his voice (e.g. Ps. 18.8, 14). Theophany was depicted in terms derived from a violent storm. At Mount Horeb in the time of Moses and again in Elijah's day the appearance of God was accompanied with the dark cloud or smoke, thunder or trumpet blast, lightning and the shaking of earth that accompanies

---

[1] For discussion of these passages with references, see most recently C. R. North, 'The "Former Things" and the "New Things" in Deutero-Isaiah', *Studies in Old Testament Prophecy* (T. H. Robinson Volume, ed. by H. H. Rowley; Edinburgh, 1950), pp. 111-126.

great thunder (Exod. 19.16 ff; I Kings 19.11-12).[1] No one could penetrate the mystery of his presence. His being was envisaged as surrounded and hidden by a cloud of smoke, or by a brilliance which had the appearance of fire. Such phenomena which surrounded and hid him from view were called his 'glory'. It was thus the 'glory' of God which descended upon the completed tabernacle and again on the temple of Solomon; it led the people through the wilderness as a pillar of cloud by day and, as it were, fire by night (Exod. 40.34-38; Num. 9.15-23; I Kings 8.10-11). Isaiah saw it in his vision (Isa. 6.4), and at the destruction of Jerusalem its departure from temple and city was the sign to Ezekiel of Yahweh's abandonment of both to defilement and destruction. Psalm 29, dominated by this nature imagery, is thought to have been originally a hymn to Baal, but borrowed and used of Yahweh.[2] It is Yahweh, not Baal, who 'maketh the hinds to calve' (Psa. 29.9), and gives the blessings of heaven (rain), of the deep (springs and rivers), of breast and womb (Gen. 49.25; Deut. 33.13 ff). Indeed, Hebrew psalmody is filled with nature images, most of them borrowed from Canaanite religion.[3]

One of the most vivid evidences of this assertion of Yahweh's complete control over nature was Israel's poetic use of the Canaanite creation myth, in which the monster dragon of chaos, Leviathan (Lotan), was slain by Baal. This unruly force was connected with the uncontrollable power of the deep and the sea. And in Israelite poetry it is Yahweh, not Baal, who has either slain the dragon or made him a faithful servant, and who controls the sea for his own purpose.[4] God's answer to Job is cast in the

---

[1] To historicize such images in such a way as to make one assume that Sinai was actively volcanic and, therefore, to be sought in Arabia (e.g. W. J. Phythian-Adams, *The Call of Israel*, London, 1934, pp. 129 ff), seems too much like translating the image, the vividly pictorial and the poetic into bold literal prose. Note the remark concerning this by Johs. Pedersen in *Israel: Its Life and Culture* III-IV (London, 1940), p. 662: 'A search might with equal justice be instituted for the mountains that melted like wax when Yahweh passed over the hills of the earth. The author has done all that he could to convey the idea of the might of Yahweh.' In Ps. 29.6 Lebanon and Sirion are said to dance like a wild bull, but this would scarcely be reason to conjure up volcanoes in their area or to move them to a volcanic area.

[2] Cf. H. L. Ginsberg, *The Biblical Archaeologist*, Vol. VIII (1945), No. 2, pp. 53-54.

[3] See John H. Patton, *Canaanite Parallels in The Book of Psalms* (Baltimore, 1944).

[4] Cf. Ps. 74.12-15, 89.9-10; Job 3.8 (read *yam*, 'Sea' for *yom* 'day'), 7.12, 9.8 (*yam* 'Sea'), 26.12-13, 38.8-11, 41; Amos 9.3; Hab. 3.8-15 (see W. F. Albright, 'The Psalm of Habakkuk', *Studies in Old Testament Prophecy*, pp. 1-18).

form of a demonstration of his power over nature; and the most spectacular evidence of that power is that God alone can control Leviathan, the symbol of the mighty destructive forces of nature (Job 41). Job, then, cannot use his own individual predicament to deny the universal evidence of the providence of God.[1]

In spite of this application to Yahweh of the natural functions of the Canaanite storm-god, Baal, images and metaphors drawn from nature were not the primary language by which he was known. The vocabulary of the nature myths of Canaan was used extensively but it was set in a historical context. Psalm 74 affirms that God who has performed such wonders in nature will surely come to the aid of his people in their distress. Yahweh's control over the sea and its monster was a language which could be historicized and used to describe the deliverance at the Egyptian Exodus; and this in turn was the ground for the hope of the new exodus in Second Isaiah (Isa. 51.9-11). Leviathan became the symbol of the historical enemies of God, who at the inception of the new age will be defeated (Isa. 27.1); and to the author of Revelation the dragon is Satan, the personification of *historical* evil, not of the destructive power of nature. In the New Jerusalem 'there shall be no more sea' (Rev. 21.1); in the light of the long history behind that word there could be few more graphic symbols for the abolition of evil in this world.[2]

Furthermore, the very anthropomorphism of the Biblical vocabulary concerning God is witness to his primary relation to history and human society. In polytheism the central and original metaphors and symbols for depicting the gods were drawn for the most part from the natural world. With the growth of social complexity the gods increasingly took on social functions, and such terms as king, lord, father, mother, judge, craftsman, warrior, and the like, were used. Yet Baal of Canaan and Enlil of Mesopotamia never shook off their primary relation to the storm which typifies nature's force. Anu, the head of the pantheon in

---

[1] Most of the older commentaries do not understand the significance of this mythological dragon and attempt to identify it with an Egyptian crocodile. The recovery of the Canaanite religious literature now enables us to grasp the deeper significance of Job 41.

[2] Cf. Howard Wallace, 'Leviathan and the Beast in Revelation', *The Biblical Archaeologist*, Vol. XI (1948), No. 3, pp. 61-68.

Babylon, originated as the numinous feeling for the majesty of the sky. He was thus given form as heaven, though subsidiary forms were the king and the bull of heaven. The mother of the gods was Ninkhursag, who arose from the feeling for the fertility of the earth and was thus given form as the earth, with subsidiary forms ascribed as mother, queen and craftsman. Ea was the sweet waters, who could be given form in the ram and the bison, but more especially as the knowing-one, the craftsman, the pundit and the wizard. Shamash was the sun who took over the function of divine judge as 'Lord Order'. Sin was the moon, who became also lord of the times, seasons, signs and portents. Ishtar was the planet Venus who typified a young maiden, somewhat spoiled and headstrong, a leader of war, a lover and wife of the vegetation-god for whom she mourned at his yearly death.

Thus the catalogue of pagan gods might continue. In the Bible, on the contrary, God is known and addressed primarily in the terms which relate him to society and to history. The language of nature is distinctly secondary. God is Lord, king, judge, shepherd, father, husband, and the like, but these appellatives are not superimposed upon a central image in nature. Nature as God's creation contains no forms on which one can focus a religious attention. The first two commandments of the decalogue make this perfectly clear. No other powers are to be associated with Yahweh as objects of worship, and a primary reason given is historical. It is because no other power was with him when he accomplished his great saving acts. He alone can and is directing the course of history (e.g. Exod. 15.11-13; Deut. 32.12, 39; Isa. 43.10-13). No images are to be made of him or of anything else in heaven or earth, for, it is affirmed, while the people heard the voice of God at Horeb, they 'saw no manner of form' on that day (Deut. 4.15). Nothing in heaven and earth may be used to picture God, but the nature of his revelation indicates his primary concern for, and relation to, man, society and history. Consequently, the only image of him possible is the mental image of a person, and the only language by which he may be addressed is drawn from the institutions of human society, as Lord, King, Father, Judge, etc. Anthropomorphism thus indicates God's personal relation to history, and to assume that we can dispense

with it as belonging to a primitive stage of our religious development is to separate ourselves not only from the Bible, but from
the Biblical conception of the true meaning of history.

IV

If the primary and irreducible assumption of Biblical theology
is that history is the revelation of God, then we must affirm that
the first inference to be drawn from this view was not concerned
solely with the power and attributes of God, but rather with the
explanation of what God had done at the Exodus. That is, the
initial and fundamental theological inference was the doctrine of
the chosen people. The use of the term 'inference' here does not
mean that Israel was consciously employing a method of reasoning
by logical deduction in the philosophical or Greek sense. The
inference was an interpretation of an event, which to Israel
became an integral part of the event and which thus could be
used for the comprehension of subsequent events. How else
could Israel explain what had happened except by a conception
of election? The God who had rescued a depressed people must
have had a reason for doing so. It is unrealistic to assume that
Israel's belief in herself as the especially chosen recipient of
Divine favour was simply the projection of the nation's egoism
or the over-compensation for an inferiority complex. How else
was Israel to account for her existence, except that God had set
his love upon her? No explanations of special spiritual or moral
merit were sufficient to explain God's action. The Divine election
was not based on merit because the leaders of the faith, at least,
constantly pointed to the faithlessness and rebellion of the nation,
which began with the murmurings in the wilderness. Israel's
greatness lay in what to the nation was a simple fact, that God
had chosen her; and God's choice rested in his own mysterious
grace. That grace was not and would not be explained; it could
only be inferred and accepted in faith and in gratitude. Evidently,
God was at work with some purpose of his own in history, and
for some reason he had chosen Israel as his special agent in
accomplishing that purpose—the weak of the earth to confound
the strong.

Once such an inference was made, it was inevitable that those who collected and edited the earliest traditions of Israel should portray all history in this light. The knowledge of the Divine election was the only means by which the Patriarchal saga could be interpreted. Thus in Genesis Abraham was the recipient of wonderful promises, repeated to each of the fathers, and his righteousness lay in his acceptance and belief in them (Gen. 15.6). The subsequent history from Moses to David marked the stages in God's fulfilment of the promises. Consequently, when the people 'sighed by reason of their bondage . . . , God heard their groaning, and God remembered his covenant with Abraham, with Isaac, and Jacob' (Exod. 2.23-24).[1]

The faith in a special election was one which always pointed forward to a future in which the full purpose of God would be manifest. The controversy of God with his chosen agent is perhaps the central theme of the Deuteronomic and prophetic writings. Yet the purpose of that controversy was not for Israel's sake alone; the agency of Israel in God's earthly programme is the deeper issue. Consequently, the prophetic eschatology is not a new invention of religious genius. It had its roots in the presuppositions of the older histories and in the attempt to interpret the work of God in the current crises of history. God's dealings with Israel were of profound significance for universal history because his revelation to Israel was the light which must some day through Israel illumine all nations,[2] and those who refused it were the enemies of God who would be destroyed before the new and final age dawned.

The doctrine of election was an inference from historical events which thus gave a peculiar meaning to nationality in Israel. Nationality was more than a collocation of people, determined by a common blood and a common soil. It was an entity which God

[1] For an analysis of the two different emphases in the literature as to the origin of the election, whether at the Exodus or at the time of Abraham, see especially Kurt Galling, *Die Erwählungstraditionen Israels* (Giessen, 1928); and H. H. Rowley, *The Biblical Doctrine of Election* (London, 1950), pp. 19 ff.

[2] For the evidence that this consciousness was at least as early as the tenth century, see the writer, *The Old Testament Against its Environment*, Chap. II; Gerhard von Rad, *Das erste Buch Mose, Genesis Kapitel* 1-12, 9 (Göttingen, 1949), pp. 14 ff, 132 ff. Contrast the very limited acceptance of this position by H. H. Rowley, *op. cit.*, pp. 65 ff, at least as regards Gen. 12.3. The popular conception of a Day of Yahweh, which is older than Amos 5.18, and the theology of kingship sponsored in the Davidic court are further factors which must be considered in this regard.

had brought into being, so that Israel was *his* people, 'a congregation of Yahweh', 'a holy nation' to whom he had imparted a measure of his own holiness by separating them to himself in the events of the Exodus (Exod. 19.6; Lev. 11.45, etc.). This special relationship to God, which was the basis of Israel's nationality, was given concrete expression more widely in the language of a legal covenant than in any other. Israel was a community held together by a solemn compact with God. Form criticism and comparative study have shown that the type of organization which distinguished Israel from other nations in the first period of the nation's history in Palestine, before the establishment of the monarchy, was that of a tribal amphictyony, an organization of tribes held together around a central shrine by a religious compact or covenant. The conception held within it the framework for political organization. God was conceived as the direct and actual ruler of the nation, so that the law, which is at the basis of all social life, was believed to be his own gift to the nation. Yahweh was thus the Lord, the King, the Judge and the Lawgiver of his people, who were his subjects or servants. He exercised his rulership by mediate means; that is, by leaders like Moses, Joshua, Gideon, Deborah whom he called for specific purposes and to whom he gave the power and the ability to fulfill their calls.[1]

Covenant thus involved a political anthropomorphism which was believed to be literally relevant for Israelite life. Under the impact of the Philistine oppression the attempt to live within it failed and a permanent form of human leadership was demanded by the people. Centralized government, however, while a political necessity was nevertheless a theological problem, for it had to be fitted into the framework of the theocratic covenant. And there were always those in pre-Exilic Israel who looked with suspicion upon the kings. To them kingship was simply God's accommodation to the needs of a sinful people who had refused to keep the covenant (e.g. I Sam. 8). The covenant theology was thus kept alive, even though as an ideal rather than as a political

[1] Cf. Martin Noth, *Das System der zwölf Stämme Israels* (Stuttgart, 1930); *Überlieferungsgeschichte des Pentateuch* (Stuttgart, 1948); *Geschichte Israels* (Göttingen, 1950), pp. 74 ff; Albrecht Alt, *Die Staatenbildung der Israeliten in Palästina* (Leipzig, 1930).

reality. As such it furnished a language which could be used to explain subsequent events. The crises of the nation were due to Israel's breach of their pledged vows; sin was rebellion, a violation of the relationship of nation to God. Therefore, God's controversy against his people, his *ribb* or legal case with the resultant sentence, judgment, or penalty was the conceptual language used by the Deuteronomists (in Deut.-II Kings) and the prophets to explain the meaning of the people's tragedies. A large proportion of the religious vocabulary of Israel was drawn from jurisprudence, and its source lay in the sense of the covenant between God and nation.

Yet behind it was the knowledge of the extraordinary grace and purpose of God, so vividly shown apart from legal merit in the Exodus and in the wilderness of Sinai. Consequently, the conception of legal penalty as an explanation of the destruction and captivity of Israel and Judah could not be envisaged as exhausting the work of God. The Exodus salvation together with the repeated triumphs through the periods of the Conquest and the Judges gave that knowledge of God which created hope, a hope that burned the most brightly in hopeless times. It was a hope which lay in history and projected a future in history, that is in human society on this earth. The relationships in the world of nature may be radically revised in the age to come, but the Bible envisages no abolition of nature as the locus for a redeemed society. The Biblical sense of the meaningfulness of history possessed a hope which could look far beyond the current history, but the final age to which God was directing events was one which had concrete substance. It was no ethereal, impersonal, substanceless existence beyond history; it was the fulfilment of history, beside which the hopes of other religions appear either as completely illusory or as quite hopeless. Consequently, while the breach of the covenant was from the standpoint of law and justice irreparable, yet because of the known grace of God the future hope could portray a 'new covenant', an 'everlasting covenant', a 'covenant of peace' (e.g., Jer. 31.31 ff; Ezek. 16.60; 37.26-27). Before the Exile the prophets seemed to believe that the punishment and judgment of God in the current historical events would in themselves bring about the inner purification of a remnant which was the necessary requisite of the new age. To Ezekiel, however, the actual situation among the captives in Babylon evidently seemed the proof that destruction and captivity does not necessarily bring about the reformation of the inner man. Consequently, God himself, he believed, would miraculously give unto the remnant of Israel a new heart and a new spirit, put his Spirit within them and cause them to walk in his statutes. Then indeed would they dwell in the land which he gave to their fathers; they would be his people and he their God (Ezek. 36.24-31). Then and only then would the fulfilment of God's purposes in the covenant be achieved.

Now to us the interpretation of the meaning of election for Israel's life in terms of a covenant is a projection of faith by means of analogical or metaphorical language. Israel inferred from the Exodus event that God had chosen her and, therefore, had established a special relationship between himself and her. This relationship, we are inclined to say, was made clear by means of the covenant ideology, drawn from patriarchal society and given an extended meaning.[1] Not so Israel, however. For her the covenant was an actual event which took place at a certain historical time and place, namely at Sinai. There God actually had demonstrated his presence to Israel (Exod. 19), so that the Deuteronomist could say that the people heard his voice though they did not see his being (Deut. 4.15; 5.22). And this, he further asserts, was a unique event which no other people had experienced (5.26). At Sinai Moses ascended into God's presence and brought down the tablets of the decalogue. There, too, God revealed to Moses the Book of the Covenant (Exod. 20.22-23.33), indeed the whole law governing the cultic and the common life (cf. Lev. and Deut.). After the law had been received, there was a formal ceremony in which the Book of the Covenant was publicly read, the people assented to its conditions, and their bond with God was sealed with 'the blood of the covenant, which Yahweh hath made with you' (Exod. 24.3-8). Thus for Israel the covenant, by which the meaning and implications of election were concretely stated, was not faith projected on history, but a real event of history which illumined the meaning of subse-

[1] So the writer, *op. cit.*

quent history and for the priestly editor of Genesis the meaning also of pre-Mosaic ages.[1]

V

From the above survey we are now in possession of the chief clues to the theological understanding of the whole Bible. There is, first, the peculiar attention to history and to historical traditions as the primary sphere in which God reveals himself. To be sure, God also reveals himself and his will in various ways to the inner consciousness of man, as in other religions. Yet the nature and content of this inner revelation is determined by the outward, objective happenings of history in which individuals are called to participate. It is, therefore, the objectivity of God's historical acts which are the focus of attention, not the subjectivity of inner, emotional, diffuse and mystical experience. Inner revelation is thus concrete and definite, since it is always correlated with a historical act of God which is the primary locus of concentration. Mysticism in its typical forms, on the other hand, subtly turns this concentration around, so that the focus of attention is on the inner revelation, while the objectivity of God's historical acts is either denied altogether or left on the periphery of one's vision. Important as Christian pietism has been in the Church, it has not escaped this subtle inversion with the result that the central Biblical perspective has been lost.

Secondly, the chief inference from this view of history as revelation was the mediate nature of God's action in history: that is, his election of a special people through whom he would accomplish his purposes. This was a proper inference from the Exodus deliverance; and the migration of Abraham to Canaan was believed to have been occasioned by a Divine call which involved election. In Genesis the election is portrayed as the goal of history and the Divine answer to the human problem. After the Exodus, it formed the background for the interpretation of Israel's life in Palestine and a central element in prophetic

[1] Cf. The priestly outline of events: The Divine command and promise to man in Gen. 1; the promissory covenant with Noah as universal man, the sign of which was the rainbow (Gen. 9); the promissory and everlasting covenant with Abraham as the representative of the chosen nation, the sign of which was the institution of circumcision (Gen. 17); and the covenant with all Israel at Sinai, the sign of which was the sabbath (Exod. 31.12-17).

eschatology and in the apocalyptic presentation of the Book of Daniel.

Thirdly, the election and its implications were confirmed and clarified in the event of the covenant ceremony at Sinai. Israel's sin was the breach of this covenant, which, therefore, enabled the faithful to see that election was not unalterable. It could be annulled by Israel herself. Consequently, covenant was something that had to be periodically renewed by ceremonies of rededication.[1] It involved the interpretation of the whole life of the people, in the social, economic, political and cultic spheres. The law of the society was the law of the covenant, given by God with the promise of justice and security within the promised land. Consequently, the central problem of Israel was envisaged as the problem of true security in the midst of covenant violation and international upheaval. This security was seen by the prophets as only to be found beyond the suffering and judgment of the Day of Yahweh. There would be a revival of the community, but only after the elect people had become scattered and dry bones (Ezek. 37).

These three elements are together the core of Israelite faith and the unifying factor within it.[2] They have little abstract or propositional theology within them. They are based on historical events and the inferences drawn from them. They cannot be grasped by the abstract rubrics of dogmatic theology. And these very same elements are the centre and core of the faith of the early church. For this reason the advent of Jesus Christ could not be understood solely or chiefly as the coming of a teacher of moral and spiritual truths. His coming was a historical event which was the climax of God's working since the creation. All former history had its goal in him because God had so directed it. All subsequent history will be directed by him because God has exalted him as Lord. In so doing he will fulfill the promises

---

[1] For a brief review of these ceremonies, see the writer in *The Old Testament Against its Environment*, Chap. II. Form criticism has led some scholars to the highly probable view that in early Israel, at least, the ceremony of covenant renewal was a yearly affair: see Gerhard von Rad, *Das formgeschichtliche Problem des Hexateuchs* (Giessen, 1938), and Martin Noth, *Überlieferungsgeschichte des Pentateuch* (Stuttgart, 1948), pp. 63 f.

[2] For the problem of the wisdom literature in this connection, particularly Job, Proverbs and Ecclesiastes, see the treatment in Chap. IV.

of God in the government of Israel, assuming the royal office of David at the right hand of God and providing the security which the sin of Israel made impossible of achievement. The election of Israel as the agent of God in universal redemption is reaffirmed in the New Israel (e.g. I Pet. 2.9-10), the Body of Christ, which is the partaker of the New Covenant in Christ's blood. In Christ God has inaugurated the new age, foreseen of old; entrance into it is by faith and by the sharing of Christ's cross, for in him our sins are forgiven and our alienation from God done away. Thus God in Christ has completed the history of Israel; he has reversed the work of Adam, fulfilled the promises to Abraham, repeated the deliverance from bondage, not indeed from Pharaoh but from sin and Satan, and inaugurated the new age and the new covenant. To be sure, the world is unredeemed and the final consummation is yet to appear. Yet Christ is the sign and seal of its coming. Hence he is the climactic event in a unique series of events, to be comprehended only by what has happened before him, but at the same time the new event which marks a fresh beginning in human history.

This, then, is the basic substance of Biblical theology. It is true that we simply cannot communicate it without dealing with the *ideas* of which it is composed. Yet to conceive of it primarily as a series of ideas which we must arrange either systematically or according to their historical development is to miss the point of it all. It is fundamentally an interpretation of history, a confessional recital of historical events as the acts of God, events which lead backward to the beginning of history and forward to its end. Inferences are constantly made from the acts and are interpreted as integral parts of the acts themselves which furnish the clue to understanding not only of contemporary happenings but of those which subsequently occurred. The being and attributes of God are nowhere systematically presented but are inferences from events. Biblical man did not possess a philosophical notion of deity whence he could argue in safety and 'objectivity' as to whether this or that was of God. This ubiquitous modern habit of mind which reasons from axioms and principles or universals to the concrete would have been considered as faithless rebellion against the Lord of history who used history to reveal his will and purpose. Hence the nearest approach to atheism which the Old Testament possesses is the fool who says in his heart there is no God (Ps. 14.1; 53.1). Yet the Psalmist means by this, not a theoretical atheism, but rather the practical atheism of a sinner who calls God's works, not his being, into question.[1] Jeremiah clarifies the point when he speaks of people in his day who refuse to believe that the great events which then are happening are the work of God. They thus 'have denied Yahweh and said: "It is not he; neither shall evil come upon us; neither shall we see sword nor famine" ' (5.12). To refuse to take history seriously as the revelation of the will, purpose and nature of God is the simplest escape from the Biblical God and one which leaves us with an idol of our own imagining.

Consequently, not even the nature of God can be portrayed abstractly. He can only be described *in relation to* the historical process, to his chosen agents and to his enemies. Biblical theology must begin, therefore, with the primary question as to why the Bible possesses the historical nature that it does. It thus must point in the first instance to this confessional recital of traditional and historical events, and proceed to the inferences which accompanied those events, became an integral part of them, and served as the guides to the comprehension of both past and future. Biblical theology, then, is primarily a confessional recital in which history is seen as a problem of faith, and faith a problem of history.[2]

---

[1] Cf. Ludwig Köhler, *Theologie des Alten Testaments* (Zweite Auflage; Tübingen, 1947), p. 1.

[2] An affirmation of Artur Weiser, *Glaube und Geschichte im Alten Testament*, p. 19, here used in a somewhat different context.

CHAPTER THREE

WHAT GOD HAS DONE

WE must now inquire further as to what portions of the Biblical recital of Divine activity in history are the most important, inasmuch as they are the clues to the remainder of the literature. In the preceding chapter the basis or core of Biblical theology was described as the deliverance from Egyptian bondage and the formation of the amphictyonic or covenant tradition at Mount Sinai, together with the conception of God, history, election, and national economy in the covenant inferred from those events. This rather narrow base needs to be broadened and supplemented, however, by the addition of other events, so that we have more than the foundation but rather the framework for the superstructure of Biblical faith. This can be done by noting the confessional use which the New Testament makes of the Old, by testing the correctness of this usage, and thus by seeing the outline or structure of Divine history as the early Church envisaged it.

I

In the New Testament we find no comprehensive treatment of the Old Testament, no unified system of doctrinal meaning, and no carefully conceived set of rules for the exegesis of specific passages. The problem of the early Church was simply to understand and to expound the meaning of Jesus Christ, his advent, life, death and resurrection. The Church thus searched the ancient Scripture for any and every clue which it contained as to what God intended, had accomplished, and would yet do, in Jesus Christ. The only data with which the Christian had to work was what Jesus himself had taught, what was contained in the acts and the accompanying words of God in the Old Testament, and what was inferred from both through the work of the Holy Spirit. It is small wonder, then, that the New Testament is filled with what to us seems at first glance to be a jumble of quotations and allusions from the Old Testament, together with occasional examples of extreme, 'unscientific' exegesis and extravagant rabbinical argument. In the past many scholars have confined their attention to this aspect of the matter, rather than to the deeper issues which alone explain it. The many-sidedness of Christ could only be comprehended and presented by many citations from the various parts of the Old Testament. Jesus Christ had come. He was not a great teacher or martyr among other teachers or martyrs; the Church recognized in him something unique and different. Consequently, he possessed a special relationship to God which other men had not had. And the method by which the New Testament writers made this clear was to envisage him as the climactic event in God's redemptive history. He is a new event; yet he can be understood only in relation to the former events which depict what God was about in his special redemptive time and which were conceived as the Divine preparation for his coming.

For this reason the person of Christ in Biblical theology is not to be comprehended solely by an analysis of his 'religious experience', nor alone by a study of his life and teaching. In him the Christian sees the revelation of God in the flesh of mortal man, but the revelation is not isolated in the one personality apart from the *historical* purposes of God. Christ is not simply the great Man, the great Martyr, the great Hero, after the general pattern of earth's heroes and martyrs. Personality in the Bible is indeed the vehicle of Divine revelation, and our concentration on history in this volume by no means is intended to minimize that fact. But unlike Confucius, Zoroaster, Mohammed, or any of the great religious leaders of mankind, the leading figures of the Bible are not to be understood solely by the analysis of their personalities, nor of the institutions and movements which they inaugurated. Indeed so uninterested is the Bible in the analysis of the inner resources and experiences of people that Biblical biographies are exceedingly difficult to prepare. Instead personality is comprehended in relation to God and to the Divinely directed history in which it is placed and called to play a responsible role. Consequently, there is no tragedy in the pagan sense, when from the human standpoint a man's work appears futile or when he is killed without just cause. God's control and direction of history means that human values are to be judged only in the light of his just purposes. Personality is God's mediate *agent* in history, a history which because of God's control reaches both backward and forward beyond itself. Hence Christ is understood, not solely as a great personality who revealed God through extraordinary inner experience, but instead as one who was *sent*, who accomplished God's work, was obedient unto death and subsequently exalted. This, then, is the meaning of the emphasis upon Christ's *coming*, instead of alone on his *being*, upon his presence in history as the new and climactic event which is to be understood only in relation to the series of Divinely directed events in the preceding history.

The one word which perhaps better than any other describes the early Church's method of interpreting the Old Testament is 'typology', ultimately derived from the Apostle Paul (cf. Rom. 5.14; I Cor. 10.6). In the words of J. Gerhard written in 1762: '*Typus consistit in factorum collatione. Allegoria occupatur non tam in factis, quam in ipsis concionibus, e quibus doctrinam utilem et reconditam depromit.*'[1] ('Typology consists in the comparison of facts. Allegory is not so much concerned in facts as in their assembly, from which it draws out useful and hidden doctrine.') In other words, typology when rightly understood and used takes historical data seriously; persons, acts and events possess a typological meaning when they are understood to have been fixed or directed by God so that they point toward the future. They possess their own original historical significance, but the eye of faith can discern that God has also set them as previews or types which point to greater and more complete facts. Allegory, on the other hand, is not primarily concerned with history but with the hidden or spiritual double meaning which its user believes he can draw out from the words or events. When allegory is used, all parts of Scripture are made to say the same thing and the significance of history is set aside. Typology has also been used in this manner so that it has become a mere branch of allegory. Yet in its proper sense it does not falsify history, but it deals with that peculiar characteristic of Biblical history in which significant events point beyond themselves to their fulfilment. They are thus types of the greater events which fulfil them.

[1] Quoted by Leonhard Goppelt, *Typos. Die typologische Deutung des Alten Testaments in Neuen* (Gutersloh, 1939), p. 8.

A few familiar examples of the typological use which the New Testament makes of the Old must here suffice. The person and the office of Jesus are seen in pure typological relation to the various offices of the Israelite covenant community, so that he fulfils them all in himself. Thus in Deut. 18.15-18, for example, Moses speaks of the office of prophet which God will later establish. In the New Testament this passage is taken to refer beyond Israelite history to Jesus (e.g. Acts 3.22-23). The words and deeds of Moses and all the prophets are interpreted as pointing beyond themselves to Christ. In the transfiguration Jesus is seen aligned with Elijah, typifying the prophet, and Moses, the giver of the law. Indeed in the Gospel of Matthew Jesus is presented as the second Moses, who gives a new law on a new mountain, who was tempted in the wilderness as Israel was tempted and who answered the tempter with the words of Moses to Israel as recorded in Deuteronomy. He alone was saved from Herod's slaughter of the children of Bethelem as Moses was saved from Pharaoh's slaughter of the Egyptian first-born. As prophet and lawgiver Jesus thus presents in final form the word and will of God. Jesus also was accorded power by God to work wonders as did Moses and the prophets before him, and in his resurrection he assumed the royal or messianic office of Israel, so that he reigns on God's right hand over the universal creation. Consequently, all the titles and functions of the Davidic king as God's son and Lord, ruler over the kingdom of God in this world, were transferred to him (e.g. Ps. 2 and 110). His atoning office is likewise explained by the Old Testament. He is the passover lamb, or the high priest who alone has access to the inner sanctuary of God, but who offers himself instead of an animal, is thus the fulfilment of Israelite priesthood and sacrifice and the true mediator between man and God. Furthermore, he is the anti-type of Adam, bringing life instead of death, the second Adam making all things new.

The Church or community of Jesus Christ is understood by means of the congregation of Israel. The community of the twelve apostles is paralleled by the twelve tribes of Israel. The Church is the heir of the election of Israel; it is the new Israel, the Israel of God, the spiritual Israel, of the seed of Abraham by adoption.

It possesses the new covenant in the blood of Christ and its festival of deliverance is the Lord's Supper, prefigured in the Israelite passover.

The events of the Exodus, the wilderness wandering and the conquest are as important for the New Testament as for the Old. In Christ is the new exodus and the new inheritance. The major portion of the vocabulary used to express the saving work of God in Christ is drawn from the Exodus event: thus the words 'redeem' and 'redemption', 'deliver', 'ransom', 'purchase', 'bondage', 'freedom'. W. J. Phythian-Adams speaks of this parallelism between Biblical events by means of the word, 'homology'. He indicates that the chief events of the Old Testament which furnish the pattern for the happenings in the New are the redemption from Egyptian bondage, the consecration of the people by covenant, and the gift of the inheritance. For example, 'when St. Paul says that God delivered us out of the power of darkness and translated us into the kingdom of the Son of love, in whom we have our redemption, the remission of our sins (Col. 1.13-14), he summarizes the Sacred Era in a single sentence. First, Redemption from bondage, followed by "translation" (the journey to the Promised Land), then consecration by the remission of sins, and finally the kingdom of "David" (the "Beloved"); the pattern is then complete. This "kingdom" in Christ is "the *Inheritance* of the saints in light".'[1] We may note further the importance of the Exodus typology in the gospel of John. After the presentation of Christ as the pre-existent word and also the completion of creation, the evangelist thinks particularly of Christ's fulfilment of the saving gifts of God in the first salvation. The controversies with the Jews which John records are largely concerned with the question as to whether Jesus does not reveal the true significance of the festivals which celebrate the Israelite deliverance and wandering in the wilderness.[2]

The problem of the New Testament use of the Old Testament is thus not one of discerning a system of principles for hermeneutics. A New Testament writer may make what appears to

---

[1] W. J. Phythian-Adams, *The Way of At-one-ment* (London, 1944), p. 23.

[2] See further in detail Harald Sahlin, *Zur Typologie des Johannesevangeliums* (Uppsala and Leipzig, 1950), and Leonhard Goppelt, *op. cit.*

us as a very forced exegesis which we should not like to imitate and from which we naturally assume that his principles of inter-pretation were most 'unscientific'. Yet just as the Bible contains no system of theology, it likewise contains no self-conscious hermeneutical methodology. To convict a New Testament writer of error or of questionable exegesis in individual passages does not in the least necessitate the assumption that his interpretative attitude and point of view were wrong. Indeed, typology, when defined as above, is more of an attitude than a precise methodology. It does not interpret according to a pre-determined set of rules in order that a unified system of meanings and a comprehensive exposition of the Old Testament may be provided. It is based very simply upon the belief that God has been directing the events of Biblical time for his own name's sake and that in Christ the whole of the former period has been brought to completion and the new age inaugurated. One of the chief differences between the Old and New Testaments is precisely at this point. The consummation of time envisaged and awaited in Israel had actually begun with the advent of Jesus Christ. To be 'in Christ' is to enter the kingdom present now, which in time to come will embrace the new heavens and the new earth when Christ will again return. Consequently, the Old and New Covenants were inevitably seen as related through the conception of preparation and promise, on the one hand, and of completion and fulfilment on the other. Thus the events of preparation were the types, the prefiguring, of the events of the new age which has dawned in Christ. The old foreshadowed the new in a typological gradation in which the new appears as new but also in which a comparison or correspondence is possible between matters in the old and the new ages.

Not only Biblical beliefs, therefore, but also Biblical hermen-eutics are determined by the peculiarly Biblical understanding of historical events as pointing toward the goal of history because they are the record of what God has done. We today find it necessary to add certain rules for the correct exegesis of Biblical passages, but it is impossible for us to discard New Testament typology without separating ourselves from Biblical faith. During the past century we have substituted for typology the naturalistic conception of growth, which means that the New Testament fulfilment is conceived in terms of purer and finer values and ideals. Typology, on the other hand, when properly defined, points to the centre of the Bible in a divinely directed, unique history wherein as a result of the fulfilment one is enabled to see that the events of the Old Testament were meant by God to be preparatory events with an inner significance only partially understood by the original participants and only to be comprehended fully in Jesus Christ.

One must affirm, however, that there is a great danger in typology if it is used as the exclusive, or even central, guide to the unity of the Bible. On the one hand, there is always the danger of playing fast and loose with historical context and meaning in order to get to the ultimate truth: that is, typology so easily slips into allegory. It may be well again to state that, properly speaking, allegory finds Biblical truth in external ideas without reference to the discipline of historical exegesis. The spiritual meaning is eternal truth unconditioned by history. Typology must always be sharply distinguished from such a procedure. The significance of an Old Testament event is to be seen at two levels, its historical meaning and its typological meaning in foreshadowing later events. Typology must thus adhere to historical exegesis while at the same time it sees a relationship between two events which God, the Director of the history, has purposely fixed so that the one is the continuation and fulfilment of the other.

On the other hand, there is an even more serious danger in a static approach to the Bible through the use of typology. While an immanent historical truth is seen as relating two or more historical events, the truth looked for may be the timeless, eternal verity or idea which is merely set within the crude frame of history. By taking off the frame we de-historicize it, even while paying lip-service to the historical context in which it is found. When thus used, typology can be more dangerous than allegory because it achieves the same end without being so openly unhistorical. It can be made into a synthesis between the Greek search for eternal truth and the Biblical concern for history. Yet Biblical 'truth' is fundamentally active; it is an interpreted act or event involving faith, decision and participation. Consequently, our interpretation must always be on the alert lest it slip into the abstract timelessness which is the subtle danger forever lurking at our steps—especially when we desire to exhibit our rational excellence.

For these reasons, typology is a dangerous exercise when elaborated systematically by any modern. It is better, therefore, that we remain confined to, and disciplined by, the chief types which the New Testament itself employs, and further that we no more attempt to use these types as material for the erection of a systematic hermeneutics than did the writers of the New Testament.

II

How do the various events align themselves together so as to provide the structure for the Bible? In other words, what precisely has God done? This can best be discerned in the earliest Christian preaching and in the Biblical confessions of faith.

Professor Oscar Cullmann in his study of *The Earliest Christian Confessions*[1] has singled out two formulae especially which were the central elements of the confessions. These are 'Jesus Christ is Lord' (I Cor. 12.3) and 'Jesus is the Son of God' (Acts 8.37; Heb. 4.14; I John 4.15). Both of the statements, it may be noted, are derived from what to the New Testament are historical acts of God. The first refers to God's resurrection and exaltation of Christ to be the reigning Lord of all creation. The second is the same, though emphasizing by means of a Davidic or royal title drawn from the Old Testament the special relationship existing between God and Christ.[2] When these statements were expanded, the expansion was almost always in the form of additions from what to the Christian were the facts of Jesus' life, death and resurrection. The Apostle Paul in Phil. 2.6-11 quotes one of the earliest confessions preserved. It is a Christian psalm which speaks of Christ emptying himself, taking the form of a servant, remaining obedient unto death, and of God's exalting him to receive the worship of all things 'that every tongue should confess that

[1] Translated by J. K. S. Reid, London, 1949.
[2] Later this title was understood, by means of the birth narratives, in another sense than it originally had.

66

Jesus Christ is Lord, to the glory of God the father'. Another common confession used in preaching was probably that quoted by Paul in I Cor. 15.3-7, which speaks of Christ's death for our sins, according to the Scriptures, of his burial and resurrection, according to the Scriptures, and of his various subsequent appearances on earth. Rom. 1.1-3 affirms 'the gospel of God (which he had promised afore by his prophets in the holy scriptures), concerning his Son, who was born of the seed of David according to the flesh, and declared to be the Son of God with power, according to the spirit of holiness, by the resurrection from the dead: Jesus Christ our Lord'.

In New Testament times there were evidently a number of such formulae, differing in wording because of the differences in occasions and personalities involved in their construction. Most of them, says Cullmann,[1] contained only the one Christological article. To believe in Christ meant of necessity the belief in the God and Father of Jesus Christ and as well in the Holy Spirit. Definitely trinitarian confessions appear more commonly after about A.D. 150, presumably because of the necessity of clearing up all ambiguity for Gentile Christians exposed to Gnosticism and not well trained in the scriptures of the Old Testament. But the central emphasis continued to be the Christological, and our interest here is to point to its objective character. What is confessed is not an internal religious or mystical feeling, nor is it a series of spiritual or moral teachings, nor a system of propositional dogmatics. It is rather the work of God in the life and death of a historical person.

The substance of the early confessions was derived, of course, from the Gospel as preached by the early Church. Dr. C. H. Dodd in his study of *The Apostolic Preaching and its Developments* (London, 1936) has attempted to isolate the central elements of the earliest Christian preaching or proclamation (*kerygma*) from the letters of the Apostle Paul and from the sermons of the Apostles as presented to us in the first thirteen chapters of the Book of Acts. This common core of the proclamation he designates as the Jerusalem *kerygma*. It was composed of at least the following elements: (1) the new age, the time of fulfilment, which God

[1] *Op. cit.*, pp. 35 ff.

67

foreshadowed by the mouth of the prophets, has actually been inaugurated by God in Christ; (2) God has accomplished this event through the ministry, death and resurrection of Jesus whose Messiahship, prophetic office (Acts 3.22), death and resurrection were all according to the Scriptures; (3) by virtue of the resurrection God has exalted Christ to his right hand as the Messianic Lord of the new Israel; (4) the actual existence and state of the Church is the proof of God's gift of the Spirit (cf. Joel 2.28 ff) and the sign of Christ's present power; (5) the Messianic age will shortly be consummated, according to God's word by the prophets, in the return of Christ; (6) accordingly, it is incumbent upon everyone to repent that God may forgive and send his Holy Spirit upon him, for in Christ God has delivered men from sin into new life.

The early preaching was thus purely confessional, possessing an objective character, based upon the inferential interpretation of the actual life and death of one who existed in history and of one whose advent climaxed, culminated, and fulfilled God's work in history. At the same time it inaugurated the beginning of a new epoch in which the Christian now lives under Christ's Lordship while awaiting the final victory which will take place at his return.

As Dodd further shows, this Jerusalem *kerygma* is the nerve centre of the New Testament and followed the lines of the summary of the preaching of Jesus as given in Mark 1.14-15: 'Jesus came into Galilee, preaching the gospel of God, and saying, "The time is fulfilled, and the kingdom of God is at hand: repent and believe the gospel".' It is impossible, Dodd shows further, to find anything in the New Testament which is more primary than the *kerygma*. We cannot think of the Gospels as the raw material from which the preaching was constructed, because the actual situation is the other way around. The Gospels themselves represent the expansion of the *kerygma* from a number of sources of tradition. None of them, therefore, are mere memoirs or biographies. They represent a new literary form unknown in the pagan world; they are 'gospels', i.e. confessional recital of historical events and traditions together with the inferences derived from the events and seen as an integral part of them. The New Testament epistles, on the other hand, are not primarily *kerygma*.

They are addressed, not to pagans, but to Christians, and their concern is with the problems which Christians faced in a pagan world. 'They have the character of what the early Church called "teaching" or "exhortation". They presuppose the preaching. They expound and defend the implications of the Gospel rather than proclaim it.'[1]

What were the chief events in the history of Israel to which the New Testament most frequently refers as the preparatory background for God's work in Christ? It is interesting to note that, while there are numerous citations, and allusions to, the Psalms and the prophets, the events most often alluded to are the great acts of God in the record beginning with Abraham and ending with David. It is curious that the New Testament does not make use of the destruction of Jerusalem, the exile, and the restoration, for those events would have completed the typological comparison of God's acts in Israelite history with his work in Christ. The Jerusalem *kerygma*, however, was content to find references in the prophets and Psalms which could be taken to refer to Jesus' death and resurrection; it did not use the exile and restoration, probably because the literature of Israel and of Judaism did not concentrate on those events in the same sense that it did on the pre-Davidic history. The tragedy of Jerusalem and Judah and the subsequent revival of a small post-Exilic community were interpreted in prophecy as the beginning of the eschatological age when God would establish his universal kingdom and redeem the whole of creation. The delay in the arrival of that consummation became a serious problem, particularly disillusioning in the failure of Zerubbabel to become the Messiah of God. The hope continued to live on and found expression in apocalyptic writings, but it was Ezra's mission to re-establish the covenant nation and to turn the people to a detailed attempt to live by the law. Prophecy as the direct interpretation of God's work in historical events died out, being replaced by apocalyptic writers, on the one hand, and specialists in the law, on the other. The New Testament cuts in behind this situation and adheres directly to the prophetic promise of the new age, though employing apocalyptic materials in so doing.

[1] C. H. Dodd, *op. cit.*, p. 9.

69

The simplest summary of the central Biblical events as the New Testament saw them is contained in the address attributed to the Apostle Paul at Antioch in Pisidia (Acts 13.16 ff). It begins in vv. 17-23 with a confessional summary of what God has done. The following are the articles of faith which it proclaims: (1) The God of Israel chose the fathers (Patriarchs); (2) he delivered their seed with uplifted arm from Egyptian slavery and suffered them in the wilderness; (3) he directed the Conquest and divided the land to them by lot; (4) after the judges, Samuel and the rejected Saul, he raised up David to be their king, as a man after his own heart who should do his will; (5) of whose seed, according to promise, he raised up a Saviour, Jesus.

The history, which this confession reviews, begins with the Patriarchs and ends with David; from that point Paul passes immediately to Jesus Christ. He thus suggests that the events from Abraham to David are the most significant history of the former times and that Christ is the continuation, the clarification and the fulfilment of the redemptive purpose of God within it. We must now turn to the Old Testament in order to see the basis upon which this selection of historical events rests.

III

Professor Gerhard von Rad has pointed out that the earliest confessions of faith which the Old Testament contains are recitals of the saving acts of God, which in expanded form provide the theme around which the historians of early Israel collected and arranged the various traditions together with the cultic, legal, poetic and other material in the early books of the Old Testament.[1] Literary criticism of the first six books of the Old Testament, the Hexateuch, has had a tendency to split them up into a great variety of literary fragments, without being able to put them back together again in such a way as to enable us to comprehend the whole. Yet this remarkable work has a theme which binds the whole together. This basic theme is somewhat as

[1] Gerhard von Rad, *Das formgeschichtliche Problem des Hexateuchs* (Giessen, 1938) and *Das erste Buch Mose: Genesis Kapitel 1-12, 9 (Das Alte Testament Deutsch,* ed. by Volkmar Herntrich and Artur Weiser, Teilband 1; Göttingen, 1949), pp. 7 ff. Cf. the review by this writer in *Journal of Bible and Religion,* Vol. XVIII. No. 4 (October, 1950), pp. 216 ff.

follows: God, who created the world, called the fathers of Israel and promised them the land of Canaan. After a long sojourn in Egypt, during which Israel had become numerous, the people were enslaved. God delivered them and led them through the wilderness by the most remarkable proofs of his grace. Finally, after a long wandering, he brought them into the promised land and gave it to them as an inheritance.

A comparison of this theme with the present contents of the books indicates only the long history of compilation in which various writers have heaped up traditional materials around the basic theme. The proper use of form and literary criticism, therefore, is not simply to atomize the contents of the books, but rather to understand the manner and the purpose in which and by which such a variety of materials have been used to expand the theme.

According to von Rad, it is possible to isolate quite a number of shorter and longer passages which indicate the source of the central elements in the theme. Especially instructive is the old confession which the worshipper was to recite when he used to bring a basket of his firstfruits to the central sanctuary, originally without doubt the tabernacle. This is quoted in Deut. 26.5-9:

> An Aramean ready to perish (wandering or lost) was my father; and he went down into Egypt, and sojourned there with a few, and became there a nation ... And the Egyptians ... laid upon us hard bondage ... And the Lord brought us forth out of Egypt with a mighty hand ... And he hath brought us into this place, and hath given us this land ...

This is more than a personal prayer of thanks; it is a confession or *credo*, which recapitulates the great saving acts which brought the community into being. A similar old confession seems to be quoted in Deut. 6.20-24:

> And when thy son asketh thee in time to come saying, What mean the testimonies, and the statutes, and the judgments, which the Lord our God hath commanded you? Then thou shalt say unto thy son: We were Pharaoh's bondmen in Egypt; and the Lord brought us out of Egypt with a mighty hand. And the Lord showed signs and wonders, great and sore ...,

71

and brought us out from thence that he might bring us in, to give us the land which he swear unto our fathers.

A third example, according to von Rad, is Josh. 24.2-13. The context is a covenant ceremony at Shechem, the significance of which may be that on this occasion various tribes and groups not involved in the original Sinai covenant joined it and adopted the Exodus traditions as the normative expression of their faith.[1] The choice which Joshua places before the people is that between Yahweh and the gods. Before presenting this choice, however, he rehearses the great acts of God in the history of the people from the time the fathers left Mesopotamia to the conclusion of the conquest. While the present form of this passage is to be dated between the ninth and seventh centuries B.C., its basic form is not a new literary creation. It bears the stamp of the old cultic *credo*, here elaborated with some freedom of expression.[2] It is the Hexateuch in miniature, in which the confessional elements emphasized are: (1) God's election of Abraham; (2) his deliverance at the Exodus; and (3) his gift of the land.

The point of this is that the earliest confessions of faith in Israel are of a certain type. They are recitals of the great saving acts of God, and they provide the clue to the typical confession which the Israelite continued to make in later ages (cf. Ps. 77.12 ff; 78; 105; 136). The confession in Deut. 26 certainly presupposes a time when the old sacral, tribal covenant, the amphictyony, was still in force; in other words, it reflects cultic practice in the period of the Judges. It lays emphasis on two central points, the deliverance from Egypt and the gift of the land. In Josh. 24, on the other hand, the election of Abraham is included, and the whole recital is the preface to the covenant ceremony. Around the theme of God's great acts in bringing the nation into being, early Israel collected all her traditions, including the various stories about the Patriarchal period and the covenant traditions of Sinai, Moab and Shechem.

The first written edition of the Hexateuchal history of which

---

[1] So Martin Noth, *Das Buch Josua* (Tübingen, 1938), pp. 108-9; *Das System der zwölf Stämme Israels* (Stuttgart, 1930), pp. 65 ff; *Geschichte Israels* (Göttingen, 1950), pp. 80 ff.

[2] That is, we must distinguish between the antiquity of such confessions and the later linguistic and stylistic form in which they now appear.

we now have knowledge was prepared by an unknown collector of old traditions who possessed an extraordinary theological profundity. He is designated by scholars as the Yahwist or J writer, whose most probable date is increasingly assumed today to be in the tenth century, during the reigns of David and Solomon.[1] In the light of his work it is evident that certain deeper dimensions have been added by him and by his predecessors[2] to the older confessions. The latter, for example, include nothing about the creation or the prehistoric period. Yet the Yahwist in Gen. 2.4b-12.9 has taken a variety of old traditions and worked them together in such a way as to portray the problem of man and his civilization. In Gen. 12.1-9, however, the primeval history is

[1] It has long been recognized that the historical allusions in J nearly all point to a period not later than the tenth century: e.g. the reference to the subjugation of the Canaanites in Gen. 9.25 which reflects what happened after the conquests of David (I Kings 9.20-21), and the ideal boundary of the nation (Gen. 15.18) which certainly reflects the claims and conquests of David (see p. 77, note 1). Consequently, R. H. Pfeiffer (*Introduction to the Old Testament*, New York and London, 1941, p. 148) can say: 'Neither J nor E makes the slightest allusion to the divided kingdom'. The only exception to this statement might be the reference to Edom securing her freedom from Israel (Gen. 27.40b), but since the work of Gunkel on Genesis this statement clearly appears as a prose addition to a poetic blessing. In any event, it need not refer to the ninth century revolt alluded to in II Kings 8.20, since Edom probably revolted after David's death and before the end of Solomon's reign (I Kings 11.14-22). More important is the fact that J represents an atmosphere of joyous security, with none of the nostalgic interest in re-creating the past for a period of crisis which pervades D, P, and the prophets. J's theme is precisely the wonderful promises made to the fathers and the marvellous manner in which God has fulfilled them in successive stages, culminating in the time of David when real security in the land was finally achieved. J exhibits no overpowering sense of sin, judgment and crisis, no repeated and insistent emphasis on the sin of idolatry, no didactic or prophetic intensity of concern for obedience to the law of God, in the sense in which these problems came to the forefront of attention during the ninth and eighth centuries. To these considerations Gerhard von Rad (*op. cit.*) has added others of great importance from his form critical study of the Hexateuch. J was a great collector of old traditions which by the time of the United Monarchy had shaken off their older cultic and aetiological connections because that was the age when the pure, naive, antique cultus of the Judge's period had entered into a crisis. The spiritual fundamentals began to change so that the old traditions were freed from their original cultic sphere. The old tribal covenant fell with the formation of the state. Thus in the Yahwist the cultic meanings have been shaken loose, and the whole has been bound together in a new way by means of the confessional recital theme found in the old cultic *credo*.

[2] Von Rad believes that the major additions to the older cultic *credo* were: (1) the building in of the Sinai tradition; (2) the filling out of the Patriarchal tradition; and (3) the introduction of the primeval traditions; and he credits these additions to the Yahwist. Martin Noth, *Überlieferungsgeschichte des Pentateuch* (Stuttgart, 1948), p. 43, observes that the first two are common to both J and E and must, therefore, have existed in the collected traditions before them both. See also the reservations in Artur Weiser, *Einleitung in das Alte Testament* (2nd ed., Göttingen, 1949), pp. 66-79.

invaded by redemptive history, and the election of Israel is presented as the answer to the problem of man. The *credo* recital is thus given a deeper dimension, for the election of Israel is set within the universal redemptive purpose of God.

Furthermore, the various cycles of Patriarchal tradition were collected around the theme of the election promises and the gracious guidance of God, of which the Exodus deliverance is represented as the first stage in the fulfilment of the promises. The traditions concerning the Sinai covenant (Exod. 19-24), which once may well have circulated independently of those narrating the great saving acts of God, were built into the overall theme as the immediate goal and purpose of the deliverance from Egypt. Having rescued Israel from slavery God bound the people to him in a solemn compact and formed them into a nation. Together with the good news of the old confession there was now the reminder of the obligation for unconditioned obedience to the will of the Divine Lord. When held together in this way, the Exodus and Sinai traditions present the two basic elements of the Biblical proclamation, the gospel and the law of God.

It is impossible today to recover the Elohist document in the Hexateuch so that we can be sure of its precise nature and extent. It exists as a series of supplementations to the basic Hexateuchal narrative, that of the Yahwist; on occasion it seems to have displaced sections of the Yahwist. There are even those today who doubt whether these supplementations can be held together and conceived as having been derived from one single document.[1] Most scholars still insist that there once existed such a thing as the Elohist document, but we have fragments of it only and these are very similar in nature to the work of the Yahwist.[2] The priestly editor or editors of the combined JE inserted considerable material of their own, including an abstract account of creation in Gen. 1.1-2.3 and an editorial framework. But their

[1] See especially P. Volz and W. Rudolph, *Der Elohist als Erzähler: Ein Irrweg der Pentateuchkritik?* (Giessen, 1933); W. Rudolph, *Der 'Elohist' von Exodus bis Josua* (Berlin, 1938); F. V. Winnett, *The Mosaic Tradition* (Toronto, 1949).

[2] Josh. 24.2-13 has usually been taken to preserve the outline of contents in the E document. Professors W. F. Albright and S. Mowinckel are inclined to the view that some of the composite material in Gen. 1-11 was actually drawn from E, though this view is not generally accepted: see *Journal of Biblical Literature*, Vol. LVII (1938), pp. 230 f; Vol. LVIII (1939), pp. 87-103.

greatest contribution was the detailed supplementation of the
Sinai covenant. They furnished a detailed description of the
tabernacle together with the forms and offices of worship associated with it (Exod. 25-31; 35-40; Lev.; and parts of Num.). The
tabernacle was the seal of God's real presence in the midst of his
people; and the priesthood and sacrificial rites were the means
ordained by him through which he might be approached and
worshipped, forgiveness of sins secured and atonement effected.
Israel's cultic affairs were thus seen as an integral part of the
covenant and fixed in the historical act of God at Sinai. Thus, for
example, the laws for the consecration of Israel's priesthood were
not given in abstract form, but in narrative form as the description
of the first consecration of Aaron and his sons. The most detailed of Israel's various laws, no matter their diverse origin,
were all tied together in the Sinai event, the original prescriptions
and as well the successive adaptations and supplementations of
them.

In the Book of Deuteronomy, the Exodus, Sinai and conquest
traditions are held together as one great series of events which
portray for Israel the nature, the will and the purpose of God, in
the light of which the meaning of the law is to be understood.
These events show the extraordinary love and righteousness of
God, to which the only adequate response on Israel's part is a
love which issues in obedience. Deuteronomy is thus a summary
of Israel's faith, based upon the gracious, saving acts of God in
election, deliverance, covenant and conquest. It is an interpretation of Mosaism placed as the introduction to Israel's history in
Palestine. Its ultimate rootage is to be traced back to the days of
the tribal covenant in the period of the Judges and to some circle
of tradition in North Israel which preserved a keen memory of
that age, though in its present form the book shows evidence of
expansion during the seventh and sixth centuries B.C.[1] In its

---

[1] See especially Gerhard von Rad, *Deuteronomium-Studien* (Göttingen, 1947). It
is not improbable that there was a close connection between the North Israelite
circle responsible for the Elohist document and that also responsible for the Deuteronomic type of material. This fact has been obscured by the tendency to ascribe
various passages in the midst of Elohist material in Exodus and Numbers to a
Deuteronomist redactor. It now seems very doubtful however, whether any
Deuteronomic editorial work was done at all on JE in the books of Gen., Exod.,
and Num. The Deuteronomic historian began with the end of Moses' life and the

light the history of Israel in Palestine, from the conquest to the fall of Jerusalem (Josh.-II Kings), was compiled as a history of the sin of the nation and its leaders who with few exceptions violated the faith. The disasters which befell the nation were thus seen as the judgment of God, who having once given his people a land, took it away again.

It is thus evident that the core of the Old Testament was a proclamation, a *kerygma*, of the great saving acts of God which brought Israel into being, in the light of which the subsequent history of the nation was compiled.[1]

IV

We have now seen that the events to which the Apostle Paul is said to have appealed in Acts 13.16 ff are precisely those redemptive acts of God to which the Israelite bore witness in his confessional recital of the works of God. They centre in the call of the Patriarchal fathers, the deliverance from bondage and the gift of the land. Yet to be added, however, is the Divine act in raising up David as a man after his own heart, of whose seed God subsequently raised a Saviour, Jesus. The figure of David in Old Testament tradition stands for the divine promise of justice, salvation and security in centralized government. David's work completed God's fulfilment of his promise of the land 'from the river of Egypt unto the great river, the river Euphrates' (Gen. 15.18-JE). The ideal boundaries of the promised land were precisely those of the Davidic empire (cf. Num. 34; Ezek. 48 and

figure of David in O.T.

conquest, evidently because in JE there existed a coherent presentation which he felt he did not need to touch. It was the priestly circle which during the exile or slightly later edited JE into the present form of the first four books as we now have them. Furthermore, P did little editing in the Deuteronomic literature (Deut., Josh., Judg., I-II Sam., I-II Kings), presumably because it was a unified block of material to which he had nothing further to add.

[1] As inferred above, the major editions of Israel's historical material were the priestly edition of JE in Gen.-Num., the Deuteronomic history of Israel (Deut.-II Kings) in Palestine which included the exposition of the meaning of the law in Deuteronomy itself (see for analysis, Martin Noth, *Überlieferungsgeschichtliche Studien* I, Halle [Saale], 1943, pp. 3-110), and the work of the Chronicler in presenting a history of Judah to the end of the 5th century B.C. (I-II Chron., Ezra-Nehemiah). While the latter had his own special interests, he was much more dependent upon D than upon P, for the Deuteronomic history was the model for his own work (so Noth, *ibid.*, p. 213 and von Rad, *Das Geschichtsbild des chronistischen Werkes*, Stuttgart, 1930).

II Sam. 8).[1] This was the territory in which the promise of
security and peace was to be fulfilled, it was hoped, under the
Davidic dynasty.

Yet it is to be observed that the oldest covenant law of Israel
made no provision for a monarchy. Deut. 17.14-20 does indeed
speak of the king and of his subjection to the law, but in form it
is a free, homiletical composition which is not based upon an
old legal statement. It has behind it, not a legal explanation of
the royal rights and duties, but a critical attitude toward the
monarchial institution. Since all of the law was conceived as a
part of the covenant relation between people and God, established at Sinai, it was prior to kingship. Centralized monarchial
government was a secondary addition to the primary acts of God
which brought the nation into being.[2]

The problem of Israel in Palestine was that of security in an
amphictyonic organization. The tribes were held together by
their sacred compact around the central sanctuary. For them the
confession of God as Lord and King was a politically relevant
statement. As the Leader of Israel God demanded loyalty,
obedience and faith. When necessary he endowed special leaders
with his Spirit, and these served until the crisis was past. Otherwise no other form of government was needed. Yet the divisive
forces of geography and idolatry weakened the amphictyonic
unity and left the people unprepared to meet outside oppression
in any vigorous manner. When the Philistine menace was at its
height, the elders of Israel demanded a king that the nation
might be organized 'like all the nations', that the king 'may judge
us . . . and fight our battles' (I Sam. 8.20). Kingship was thus a
political necessity, adopted in direct imitation of the pagan nations.
The amphictyonic organization was a unique expression of the
covenant theology; monarchy was a foreign, a borrowed insti-

---

[1] The river of Egypt was, of course, the *Wadi el-'Arish* in the Sinai Peninsula.
Undoubtedly David laid claim to the desert country reaching toward the Euphrates
as did the king of Zobah whose territory in eastern Syria he conquered (II Sam. 8.3).
It is probable, however, that his actual administration border on the north was that
given in Num. 34.7-12 and Ezek. 48.1: see G. E. Wright and F. V. Filson, *Westminster Historical Atlas to the Bible* (Philadelphia, 1945), Pl. VII, A. and K. Elliger,
'Die Nordgrenze des Reiches Davids', *Palästina-Jahrbuch*, 1936, pp. 34 ff.

[2] See further Martin Noth, *Die Gesetze im Pentateuch* (Halle [Saale], 1940),
pp. 9-15.

tution, which created a problem of theological accommodation
to the covenant faith.

In the Jerusalem royal court, especially in the time of David,
an elaborate attempt was made to fit the royal office into the
historical purpose of God in the election of Israel. For one thing,
the king was anointed with holy oil, hitherto reserved for the
priestly office. This oil was specially prepared and to be used for
sacred purposes only (Exod. 30.22-32). When poured on the
priests and the paraphernalia of worship, a 'cleansing' occurred,
for anointing and hallowing went together. When taken over for
the royal office the person of the king was consecrated and hal-
lowed by the rite for the divinely appointed office. He was thus
separated from ordinary people; he was 'Yahweh's Anointed'.
In the cases of Saul and David anointing was also accompanied
by the special gift of the Spirit (I Sam. 10.1, 10; 16.12-13).

After the Divine rejection of Saul, dynastic succession was
established with David and his descendants. This dynasty was
specially elect of God, and accompanying the election were the
Divine promise and covenant (II Sam. 7.8-29; 23.5; I Kings
8.22-26; Ps. 89.3-4, 19-37). God granted enduring power and
stability to the throne; and the king was to fulfil the purposes
for which the power was given; namely, to provide justice and
security. In several of the Psalms the relation of God and king
is clearly seen.[1] These Psalms are those which, among others,
Christians traditionally have interpreted messianically. They are
indeed messianic, but not in the usual sense of the term. Originally they probably did not refer to a future king provided by God
in the new age. Rather they were hymns composed for use in
certain temple services in which the king was the focus of attention (e.g. at a coronation, a royal marriage, etc.). They thus depict
in ideal form the role which the king was to play in God's
purposive historical activity. From Psalms 2 and 110, for example,
we infer that the king could be conceived as God's 'son', his
vice-gerent, endowed with his power; he would rule until all
God's enemies in the earth were subdued. The king was the

[1] E.g. Ps. 2; 18; 20; 21; 45; 72; 89; 101; 110; 132: see Hermann Gunkel and
Joachim Begrich, *Einleitung in die Psalmen* (Göttingen, 1933), pp. 140-171; Elmer A.
Leslie, *The Psalms* (New York and Nashville, 1949), pp. 62 ff.

embodiment of his people, and the universal kingdom which God would establish would see the exaltation of the king, and therefore of the people, over all the nations of the earth.

It is quite clear, however, that the pretensions of this Davidic or royal theology were not universally accepted in Israel without qualification. The prophetic evaluation of kingship was customarily negative. In I Sam. 8, for example, the monarchy is said to have been permitted, and the king chosen by God, as the Divine concession to human weakness and sin. God gave the people a king solely because their faithlessness made it impossible for them to find security under God's direct rulership. Yet in accepting kingship the people were warned to expect the royal misuse of power, and the terms used were descriptive of what actually occurred during Solomon's reign (cf. also Deut. 17.14-20). Indeed, it was true during the subsequent centuries that the royal office was badly misused and few of the rulers could be said to have been faithful to their consecration. Consequently, neither the Deuteronomic corpus of literature (Deut.-II Kings) nor the prophets deal at length with the royal theology which we know must have been fostered in the royal court of the Davidic dynasty in Jerusalem. Yet God's promise or covenant with that dynasty was remembered, and those Judean prophets who were familiar with the royal court took it up into their prophecies. Isaiah, Micah, Jeremiah, Ezekiel, Haggai and Zechariah speak of the Anointed (Messiah) of Yahweh, or of the Branch from the Davidic stock, but they shift the basic reference from the current king to the ruler whom God is about to provide in the eschatological age. In this divinely sent king will lie complete security and justice; he will be endowed with the Spirit and power of Yahweh; his reign will accompany the new and everlasting covenant of peace; and his dominion will be from sea to sea, and from the river Euphrates to the ends of the earth.[1] The promises accompanying the Divine act in raising up David as king now become an integral part of prophetic eschatology. The new David whom God will provide is seen over against the current or previous kings, most of whom had betrayed their consecration with the

---

[1] Cf., e.g., Isa. 9.6-7; 11.1-5; Micah 5.4; Jer. 23.6; 33.15-16; Ezek. 37.21-28; Hag. 2.21-24; Zech. 6.9-14; 9.9-10.

result that the judgment of God fell both on them and the people through the medium of historical crises and oppression.

The story of Israel after David's time was thus viewed by its interpreters as chiefly one of sin and judgment. Consequently, the early Church could view the rejection and crucifixion of Jesus with deeper understanding since it was possible to identify the generation responsible for Jesus' death with the earlier generations responsible for the rejection of God's word through Moses and the prophets (e.g. Acts 7.51-53). Furthermore, the most notable saving acts of God in Israel were seen concluded in David, only to be renewed again in Jesus Christ, who is in truth the new David long awaited. The figure of David was thus projected into the historical hope of Israel, which to the early Church led directly to Christ who fulfilled it.

Christ: the new David [margin annotation]

The Davidic office of Christ, however, was assumed only when God raised him from the dead. It did not exhaust the meaning of his life and death, which fulfilled also Israel's redemptive and vicarious mission as envisaged especially by Second Isaiah. The latter's suffering servant, despised and rejected but vicariously bearing the sins of the world, was not a messianic figure in the technical sense of the word. He was a 'corporate personality' by which the prophet explained the meaning of the historical tragedy of the nation's destruction and exile. The figure of the righteous sufferer can scarcely be said to have been drawn from the royal theology of the Davidic king.[1] He is the antithesis of royalty; he possesses no kingly insignia, no glory and honour, no power for the leading of armies or wars. According to Second Isaiah, it is the Persian emperor, Cyrus, who has been given power to

[1] The attempt has been made to reconstruct a New Year's festival in Israel, moulded after one in Babylon in which at the beginning of each year the king ritually re-enacted the divine battle at the beginning of time against the forces of chaos. In this ritual the king underwent a humiliation before the final victory. In Israel, it is felt, this yearly festival was historicized in the temple services conducted by the Davidic dynasty, so that the enemies were the historical enemies of God, rather than the dragons of chaos. If so, then Isaiah 53 may have been drawn from a royal ritual, in which the humiliation of the king was the preliminary of his exaltation by God: cf. Ivan Engnell, 'The Ebed Yahweh Songs and the Suffering Messiah in Deutero-Isaiah', *Bulletin of the John Rylands Library*, Vol. 31, No. 1 (Jan., 1948), pp. 3 ff. For my part, I can only say that the evidence adduced for such an interpretation of the suffering servant is so meagre, tenuous and strained that the theory is most difficult to accept: see further Aage Bentzen, *Messias, Moses redivivus, Menschensohn* (Zürich, 1948), pp. 42-71.

function as Yahweh's anointed king (Isa. 45.1-4).[1] It is Cyrus, who for Yahweh will make the crooked straight, break the bars of iron, and open the treasures of secret places. The servant, by contrast, has a redemptive, vicarious, prophetic and pacific role to fill among the nations, though to be sure he, like Moses, will lead his people in a new exodus. His is a salvation apart from the wielding of power unless in the Mosaic manner, and it will mean the pouring out of his 'soul' unto death, though in so doing God will divide for him a portion with the strong (Isa. 53.12). Second Isaiah thus separated the royal and the redemptive missions of Israel, applying the former to the pagan Cyrus and confining Israel for the most part to the latter. In Jesus Christ, however, the two are again brought together. In his life and death he was the prophetic, vicarious sufferer for the sins of the world, but following his resurrection he was exalted by God to the royal office, in which he reigns, not from an earthly but from a heavenly throne on the right hand of God.

The chief events of the redemptive history of the acts of God are thus precisely what the confessional summary of Acts 13.17-23 says that they are. Christ is the fulfilment of this history, both of the promises to Israel as a whole and to David the king. He is now the reigning Lord, but God's work in him is not yet completed, and will not be until his second advent in the redeemed and universal kingdom.

V

Numerous questions now present themselves, and to at least a few of them we must here address ourselves. The contention thus far has been that Biblical theology cannot be analyzed after the manner of propositional dogmatics because it rests on a living, changing, ever expanding and contracting attitude toward historical events. Biblical man, living within a certain historical continuum, was aware that events were not really understood except as they were searched for the revelation they contained of what God was doing and what he willed. History thus could not

[1] It is difficult to accept the view of those who follow C. C. Torrey (*The Second Isaiah*, New York, 1928, pp. 38-52) in regarding this Cyrus passage as a reinterpretation of an original which did not possess the name. A redactor, in this view, has radically altered the prophet's original meaning.

be conceived as a secular, naturalistic, cause-and-effect process in which events are to be explained solely by the interplay of environment and geography on individual and social organisms. Happenings become history when they are recognized as integral parts of a God-planned and God-directed working, extending from creation to the eschaton. Each individual event has historical significance only when it is taken into and used by this supra-individual, purposive activity.[1]

The clue to the meaning of history, as the Bible conceives it, is a particular proclamation, a *kerygma*, of the great redemptive acts of God which have been outlined above. Yet there is more to history than the spectacular saving events which furnish security, comfort and hope. History is also, perhaps more so, filled with suffering, tragedy, death, defeat, war, destruction, insecurity and disillusionment. Consequently, Biblical man recognized the anger as well as the love of God, his function as Judge as well as Redeemer. Nevertheless, the *kerygma* proclaimed his saving acts as the clue even to the meaning of tragedy, war, and suffering. History never escapes God's hand, its terrors never mean that he is unjust; his anger never conflicts with his love. The grace of God as affirmed in the *kerygma* was the inescapable inference from his redemptive acts. Consequently, even war is a part of his gracious activity; the 'day of Yahweh' is the first stage of redemption. He uses sinful human agents as the instruments of his righteous judgment in history, though they may not recognize the fact that they are his agents, so that the selfish imperialism of men is employed by God to his own ends. Nevertheless, in the Biblical view this does not mean that the responsibility of man for his own acts is removed, nor does it mean that God is unrighteous. There is always an element of mystery in God at this point, but Biblical man simply recognized what to him were simple facts: namely, that the primary acts of God were redemptive and reveal his saving purpose throughout all history (consequently, God is both Sovereign and good), and that his acts of

---

[1] Cf. Artur Weiser, *Glaube und Geschichte im Alten Testament*, p. 20. Weiser weakens his case, however, by his use of the word 'spiritual' for this supra-individual meaning; he thus unwittingly throws his argument out of definite focus into a generalized, diffuse, 'spiritual' continuum above the human sphere, which lacks the driving, compelling solidity and definiteness of the Biblical viewpoint.

judgment were the just penalty on sin (consequently, man's response to God's will is a matter of responsible choice).

The prophets were primarily interpreters of history in this light. They were not teachers of general religious truth; they were the heralds of God, and their 'Thus saith the Lord' explained God's intention and meaning in the events of their day. The source of their enlightenment was not from mystical experiences but from history itself and from the character and purpose of God revealed in both past and present. To be sure, Moses and Isaiah, like the Apostle Paul, had visions at the beginning of their careers, and these might be described in terms of religious experience; but such experiences were concerned with the call to a particular vocation which involved a complete change in their previous habit of life. They did not appeal subsequently to such experience as the source of their message. The Word which came to them interpreted events, and they were not concerned to deal publicly with their experience. The work of God which they expounded was more objective; it was exterior to that with which mystical experience customarily deals.

The Christian Church—especially those communions of the Church which trace their lineage to the Reformation—speaks of the Bible as 'the Word of God'. Yet when this phrase is interpreted to mean that the centre of the Bible is a series of divinely given teachings, then it is certainly a misconception and its use a disservice. The Bible indeed is filled with the words of God. The prophets proclaimed God's Word, not their own. The Word, however, is not an abstraction which can be presented in a systematic theology. It accompanies historical events. It is obvious that such events need interpretation before their true meaning can be understood. Consequently, when God acted, he also 'spoke' in numerous ways, but especially by chosen interpreters. Even the law as the Word of God was rooted in the Sinai covenant and was historically conditioned. It does not give timeless prescriptions for actions, as the casuistry of the Rabbinical Period in attempting to make the original laws fit every conceivable situation so vividly shows. The same is true of the prophetic Word, with the result that the great variety of attempts to apply it literally, especially in the apocalyptic wing of the

Church, have always met with difficulty, since situations are never completely identical and since history never repeats itself in exactly the same way. Furthermore, if a prophet were accused of proclaiming a false Word, he could only rely upon the future action of God for confirmation (cf. I Kings 22.28; Jer. 28.5-9). The situation in the New Testament is quite similar. To speak of the Divine work in Christ as the Word of God means that like the Evangelist John we must reinterpret radically what we mean by the Word. John's Gospel speaks of the Word becoming flesh and dwelling among us. In other words, the Word is a Person who lived in history, not a system of ideas or teachings, nor even an abstract principle in the Greek sense. It is the occasion and the accompaniment of God's action in history, which attains its ultimate form in the historical person of Christ.

In dealing with Biblical theology, therefore, primary attention must be given, not to abstractions concerning the nature of God, but to history. This involves the use of all our tools for historical criticism, for if we fail to take history every bit as seriously as the Biblical writers, we shall not be expositors of Biblical faith. Yet history has a special sense in the Bible. While dealing with actual events and traditions, Biblical history is centred in its Creator and Director. By means of human agents God provides each event with an accompanying Word of interpretation, so that the latter is an integral part of the former, and both together serve as the guide to the understanding of future events. God is thus known by what he has done. The so-called 'attributes' of God are inferences drawn from the way he has acted. His righteousness, justice, love, grace, jealousy, and wrath are not abstractions with which we are free to deal abstractly—that is, apart from history. They are all descriptive of the way God has directed history; and hence it is inferred that they all find their unity in him. Unlike the Canaanite Baal who was the embodiment of nature's cycle and thus could be acclaimed as alive only because during the summer he was dead, Yahweh is 'the living God' because he is continually and eternally at work with his creation. He is, therefore, external to the processes of his creation, while at the same time revealing his purpose and will within them. He, then, is God, not a creature, and consequently he is 'holy'. The 'attribute'

84

of holiness simply refers to that mystery in the Divine being which distinguishes him as God. It is possessed by creatures and objects only in a derived sense, when these are separated by God himself to a specialized function. Of all the Divine 'attributes' holiness comes the nearest to describing God's being rather than his activity. Yet it is no static, definable 'quality' like the Greek truth, beauty and goodness, for it is that indefinable mystery in God which distinguishes him from all that he has created; and its presence in the world is the sign of his active direction of its affairs.

Since God is known by what he has done, the Bible exists as a confessional recital of his acts, together with the teaching accompanying these acts, or inferred from them in the light of specific situations which the faithful confronted.[1] To confess God is to tell a story and then to expound its meaning. Is Biblical theology solely concerned with abstractions of the meaning, or must it be as primarily concerned with the story as were the Biblical writers? Obviously, it must be both at the same time, for the abstractions cannot be separated from the history. They are inferences from the history and are always subject to deepening and correction in the light of the history. The nearest the Bible comes to an abstract presentation of the nature of God by means of his 'attributes' is an old liturgical confession embedded in Exod. 34.6-7 and quoted in part in many other passages:[2]

> Yahweh, Yahweh, a compassionate and gracious God, slow to anger, abundant in *ḥesed* [gracious loyalty to the covenanted promises] and fidelity, keeping *ḥesed* for thousands, forgiving iniquity and rebellion and sin, though by no means acquitting (the guilty), visiting the iniquity of the fathers upon the children and upon the children's children unto the third, even the fourth (generation).

The emphasis in this confession is upon the gracious, loyal and forgiving nature of God, an emphasis which lies at the centre of

[1] The wisdom literature and many of the Psalms do not fall into this description of the chief characterizing elements of Biblical literature. Their relation to this statement will be dealt with in Chapter IV.

[2] E.g. Exod. 20.5-6; Num. 14.18; Deut. 5.9-10; 7.9-10; II Chron. 30.9; Neh. 9.17, 31; Joel 2.13; Jonah 4.2; Ps. 86.15; etc. This confession is one of the very few in the Bible which is not a recital of events.

the Biblical *kerygma*. Yet this Divine grace is a two-edged sword which appears in the human scene as a power working both for salvation and for judgment that salvation may be accomplished. We should note, however, that every statement of the confession is inferential. We know God is like this because it is what we infer from what he has done. Consequently, we may safely use these inferences in our struggle to understand what he will do in the time to come.

CHAPTER FOUR

WHAT MAN HAS DONE

WE now turn to the Biblical teaching regarding man. Yet here again we find difficulty in systematizing the data, because the Bible is no more a textbook or treatise on anthropology than it is on the being of God. What is known about man is inferred from the way he acts in response to the activity of God. God's creation of man is followed by a story of what man did in Paradise. Man's creation of civilization is accompanied by stories depicting his alienation from God. The election of Israel and the murmuring of Israel go hand in hand. God created the nation and gave it a land, but the people went whoring after other gods and lost the land. God raised up David as a man after his own heart; yet David in lust misused his power to kill Uriah and obtain Bathsheba. God sent his prophets, most of whom were content to steal their message 'every one from his neighbour' (Jer. 23.30), and the few who did speak God's Word were scarcely heeded. God sent a Saviour of the seed of David, but the people crucified him and one from his own inner circle of disciples betrayed him. In the risen Christ God established his redeemed community, the Church, which promptly split into factions. God's act was always a challenge to decision and commitment, and man's response the portrayal of his inner state.

What kind of being is it that God has created and with whom he has chosen to deal? The obvious inference from the record of what man has done is that such dignity as he has arises from the fact that God has chosen to have communion with him, that God has set value upon the works of his hands, has called him to the task of obedient servitude, and has seen fit graciously to direct his history. The focus of attention is not on man's inherent or natural dignity and value because his works exhibit the very reverse of dignity and a betrayal of value. It is rather the mysterious grace of God in confronting man with a Divine will and a responsible task which is the source of the Bible's estimate of man's worth. The keynote is struck by the familiar eighth Psalm:

The God who has set his splendour above the heavens, and from the weak has established strength against his enemies, brings forth the Psalmist's question as to what man is that God has chosen to be mindful of him and visit him. The poet has no answer to his question. It is the mysterious goodness of God which has crowned man with glory and honour and put all earthly creation under his dominion.

The Bible's estimate of the work of man is thus derivative from its view of the meaningfulness of history. God has been mindful of man, has visited him, and has placed him as king over the world—what other inference can be drawn from God's direction of human history? Furthermore, the very fact of God's visitation presupposes a capacity given man which enables him to respond, to understand, to receive a knowledge of God, and to accept the Divine command to rule the earth. Man alone among the creatures of earth is able to receive and act upon God's visitation. Consequently, there exists in man a relatedness, a similarity, a likeness, an 'image' of God. This does not mean that man is in any sense Divine or that he possesses any portion or 'spark' of the Divine being within him. He is a creature of earth, made of the earth, though vitalized by God (Gen. 2.7) and set at the head of creation. Yet he has the capacity to receive God's revelation, to act responsibly in obedience to God and to rule the earth as a king. The priestly writer of Gen. 1 can only infer from this that man was created with a resemblance or image of God in him.[1]

image Dei

[1] 'Image' and 'likeness' in Gen. 1.26 are thus highly metaphorical expressions, and are not subject to the subtle, highly rational distinctions frequently imposed upon them: e.g. the opinion of the Church of the early centuries and of the Middle Ages that the two words refer to separate attributes of man, such as rationality and freedom of the will on the one hand (image), and original righteousness or spiritual communion on the other (likeness); or the scholarly discussion as to whether the words refer to a corporeal or spiritual resemblance between man and God. The latter argument is quite irrelevant in view of the psychology which Biblical man shared with the whole pre-Greek world. There was no separation of body and soul, and man was conceived as a unified psycho-physical organism in which the psychical functions of the *ego* were conceived as finding expression in the various parts of the body. In attempting to express the idea of a resemblance between the being of God and the being of man by means of the metaphor 'image', the Biblical writer was scarcely conscious either of the difficulties or of the distinctions that occur to us in discussing the question. Certainly the Biblical view of man 'as an animated body and not as an incarnate soul' (H. Wheeler Robinson) is much nearer to modern psychological opinion than is that of the Greeks. Yet while the Hebrews had no

The Bible never pauses to reflect systematically on the meaning of this Divine resemblance or image in man. It is simply stated as an inference from God's creative activity and then dropped. Furthermore, it may perhaps be wondered that the Bible does not contain many more expressions concerning man's glory and honour, inasmuch as he is the lord of creation and, according to Gen. 1-2, the aim and the climax of God's creative work.[1] Seldom do the Psalmists thank God for the nobility and honour of man. The few expressions which do occur, as in Ps. 139.14 ('I will praise thee; for I am fearfully and wonderfully made: marvellous are thy works'), never envisage man as an independent object of reflection. It is rather man in relation to God, man's creation as a work of God, man's utter dependence upon the continued activity of God, which furnish the context for the understanding of the worth of man. Biblical man thus does not attempt to understand himself by means of the world of nature, but solely in his relationship to God. Biblical anthropology, accordingly, cannot be treated solely as an independent subject; the knowledge of man is impossible apart from the knowledge of God. And the word 'knowledge' in this sense does not refer to a coherent body of truth; instead it refers to the nature of a person who is known in and by his relationship to the Divine Person. Biblical knowing is an event in the intercourse between two personalities. The priority, of course, belongs to God who communicates himself by revelatory happenings and establishes the relationship between man and himself. Man's knowledge of his own nature is obtained from his act of decision as well as from his contemplation of God's works in relation to him. This conception of knowledge is very different from that which we normally hold. In the latter,

conception of pure being in spiritual terms apart from material form, it is highly improbable that the author of Gen. 1 was primarily concerned with the superficial rather than the deeper aspects of personal being. There is always the danger of reading more into a metaphor than was intended: cf. W. Eichrodt, *Theologie des Alten Testaments*, Teil 2 (2nd impression, Berlin, 1948), pp. 60 ff; Gerhard von Rad, *Das erste Buch Mose* (Göttingen, 1949), pp. 44 ff; Kurt Galling, *Das Bild von Menschen in Biblischer Sicht* (Mainz, 1947); Friedrich Horst, 'Face to Face', *Interpretation*, Vol. IV (1950), pp. 259 ff; etc. The most recent treatment of Hebrew psychology is that of Aubrey R. Johnson, *The Vitality of the Individual in the Thought of Ancient Israel* (Cardiff, 1949).

[1] Cf. Karl Barth, *Die Lehre von der Schöpfung* (*Die Kirchliche Dogmatik* III 1 Zürich, 1945), pp. 20 ff.

knowledge is not primarily concerned with revelation and decision but with our seeing or understanding of something which was always there awaiting our perception.[1]

Professor Emil Brunner has pointed so clearly to this characteristic nature of Biblical theology:

> The Bible says nothing of a God as He is in Himself and nothing of a man as he is in himself, but only of a God who from the first is related to man and of a man who from the first is related to God, and, indeed, in such a way that in this relation God is inconvertibly the first, man inconvertibly the second. This is to say that God is the Creator-Lord and man is the creature, created to be freely obedient.[2]

Moreover, it is likewise characteristic of the Bible that

> this two-sided relation between God and man is not developed as doctrine, but rather is set forth as happening in a story. The relation between God and man and between man and God is not of such a kind that doctrine can adequately express it in abstract formulas ... It is not a timeless or static relation, arising from the world of ideas—and only for such is doctrine an adequate form: rather the relation is an event, and hence narration is the proper form to describe it. The decisive word-form in the language of the Bible is not the substantive, as in Greek, but the verb, the word of action ... God 'steps' into the world, into relation with men ... He acts always in relation *to them*, and He always *acts*.
>
> Similarly, men are ... those who from the first are placed in a specific relation to God and then also place themselves in such a relation: either positive or negative, obedient or disobedient, true or false, conformable to God or impious. They too are always considered as those who act: and their action, whether expressing sin or faith, is always understood as action in relation to God.[3]

The Biblical interest in man is thus not in man's *nature*, but in what he has done; and what he has done is understood as his response to or over against the action of God. It is difficult,

---

[1] Cf. especially Emil Brunner, *The Divine-Human Encounter* (Philadelphia, 1943), Chap. 2.
[2] *Ibid.*, pp. 58 f.   [3] *Ibid.*, pp. 47 f.

therefore, to speak of a Biblical doctrine of the nature of man, except when doctrine is conceived in terms of theology as recital.

II

Christian theology in dealing with anthropology has tended to confine itself very largely to the priestly writer's phrase, 'in the image of God' (Gen. 1.26-27), and the Yahwist writer's portrayal of Adam's fall (Gen. 3), on the one hand, and, on the other hand, to the redemption wrought by God in Jesus Christ as the second and life-giving Adam. The outline of the subject is thus drawn chiefly from Gen. 1-3 and the letters of Paul: (1) The nature of man as God created him; (2) the nature of man as a 'fallen' creature, inheriting a capacity for sin from Adam; and (3) the doctrine of the atonement in Christ. It is, of course, impossible to treat either the first or second apart from Christ. All Christian doctrine has its centre in him. Hence in any treatment of man in God's image the New Testament presentation of Christ as the true man of God must be central (e.g. II Cor. 4.4; Col. 1.15). The relationship between the Son of Man and the Father depicts man as he should and was intended by the Father to be. At the same time, the reception, treatment and crucifixion of the Saviour reveals more vividly than anything else man's 'fallen' and rebellious nature, while the atonement is God's act in Christ to forgive, redeem and recreate man. The sin and death in Adam have placed a barrier between man and God which Christ as mediator has removed. It is this act of God's grace which restores the original creation (e.g., Rom. 8.29; Col. 3.10; I Cor. 15.49; II Cor. 3.18). Consequently, the Cross is the only adequate symbol of Biblical faith, since in it the righteousness of God is truly presented in both its aspects of judgment and of salvation, as also man's sin and redemption.

There can be no doubt that the three-fold outline given above does indeed fix upon a central emphasis of the Bible. Under it, perhaps as well as under any other, the Biblical understanding of man might be treated. The difficulty with it is that too much emphasis is placed on what Brunner calls the 'substantive', or the existing, inner being of man as a definable object of analysis. Thus Christian discussion of the phrase, 'image of God', has tended to lay considerable emphasis upon man's natural faculties, his reason, his freedom of will, his spirit, his immortal soul, his psychological attributes, etc. This type of discussion is entirely legitimate in a Christian philosophy, but it scarcely can be called 'Biblical theology'. It is taking an unexplained and undefined statement of the priestly editor of Genesis as a symbol which is capable of expansion in ways not considered by the original writer or by any subsequent Biblical author.[1]

Similarly, Christian treatment of the 'fall' of man has continually been in danger of losing the active, living and vital relationship between God and man, one which can only be depicted by narration, for a static view of man's nature as totally depraved and alienated from God. The subtlety, the flexibility and the warmth of the Biblical story of man's acts is thus in danger of being lost by translation into a rigid, formal, inflexible and cold postulate, which amidst the changing situations of life raises intellectual difficulties. Not that this translation is totally wrong, but that it attempts to change the story, in which we see ourselves mirrored, into a universal, abstract, impersonal rationalism. Our attention is immediately turned by it from vital and responsible self-understanding and active decision to intellectual cogitation and rational argumentation. The Bible gives no philosophical treatment of human depravity. Is man totally or only partially depraved? Is his difficulty due to an *innate* moral corruption and tendency to evil, or is it due to his misuse of free choice in following the bad example of Adam? (Augustine *versus* Pelagius.) Is he predestined to salvation or destruction, the recipient or non-recipient of irresistible grace, or does he have the capacity in himself to accept or reject election, to accept or reject the grace? (Calvinism *versus* Arminianism.) The Bible gives no clear, distinct and incontrovertible answer to these questions because they represent an intellectual cogitation on man as a 'substantive' and because they shift the focus of attention from flexible, moving

---

[1] Calvin's treatment of the *Imago Dei* seems to me to be a case in point. While expressing an essentially Biblical viewpoint, it nevertheless defines the phrase with vastly extended meanings unknown to the Bible: for summary see T. F. Torrance, *Calvin's Doctrine of Man* (London, 1949), Chaps. 3-6. Yet in defence of Calvin it must be said that he is reacting against the scholastic faculty-psychology in order to present a more Biblical view of man's nature in relation to God.

narration which is the mirror of human life to a systematic, propositional dogmatic. The dynamic movement of the Bible is formalized into a rational paradox, which the mind naturally tries to resolve by taking one side or the other.

Furthermore, Christian theology has often tended to think of man's knowledge of sin as gained through the law which enables man to see himself as he really is over against what he should be. The answer to Question 14 of the Westminster Shorter Catechism states that 'sin is any want of conformity unto, or transgression of, the law of God'. Even Melanchthon defined sin as 'a depraved affection, a depraved motion of the heart against the law of God'.[1] Yet the danger in such an exclusive emphasis is always a forensic view of sin which obscures what the Biblical narration makes so clear: namely, that all sin is against God himself and not against a formal, legal postulate. Just as all Biblical worship is either idolatrous or else directed solely to God (and in the New Testament also to Christ) but to no other being in heaven or earth, so also sin is primarily a violation of our personal relationship with God. To be sure, the Reformers saw and emphasized this point with especial clarity over against the teaching of the Medieval Church, but the danger of over-simplifying the Bible through abstract propositions remained and is especially evident in the post-Reformation period. The roots and occasions of sin in the Bible are as various as life and history are varied. Much more is involved than law alone.

Moreover, it is doubtful whether it can be maintained from the Biblical narrative that man's knowledge of sin is brought to light solely by the law. Biblical history depicts the acts of God, man's acts in response, God's work in response to that of man, etc. It is a movement in the context of events, and frequently man is not fully aware of his sin until God's subsequent act of judgment. It is not law alone which brings knowledge of sin, though to be sure law was conceived as the historical expression of God's will. It is especially God's acts of grace and judgment which bring the true nature of man's acts and the motives behind them to attention. To define sin as primarily violation of law so intellectualizes and formalizes its nature that the personal, active

[1] C. L. Hill, *The Loci Communes of Philip Melanchthon* (Boston, 1944), p. 82.

movement of Biblical history is placed in the background, out of focus, even when not denied.

III

How, then, shall we treat the Biblical material relating to man? It would appear that we can do so, not by asking the abstract question as to what man is in himself, but by simply observing what he does in the great variety of situations which he faces in history and what the effects on his actions are.

Yet the Biblical preface (Gen. 1-11) indicates that we must begin with certain assumptions about man in the world which are inferences derived from reflection upon the history of the Divine-human activity as a whole. The righteous nature of God as revealed in the *kerygma* means that no pessimistic view of the evil of the world is to be permitted. The creation of God is good because God is good. Yet it is quite obvious that the life of man as known in history is not an unmitigated good. It is typical of the Bible that it does not seek to explain this situation as much as it simply attempts to describe it in narrative form. The time is placed in the prehistoric age, because history is really conceived to begin with God's redemptive act in the election of Abraham. The materials used are old traditions of heterogeneous origin, employed in such a way as to illuminate not alone the prehistoric age as it was conceived from the available traditions but also the situation of all men and nations in history.

Everything in man's current life is the antithesis of God's intention for him as revealed in the story of the Garden of Eden. Man's existence is now a continual struggle with temptation (the serpent; Gen. 3.15) on the one hand, and with the earth for livelihood on the other. The pain and struggle we undergo are due to the fact that God has cursed, not ourselves as living beings, but the nature with which we now must constantly strive and in which we are placed (Gen. 3.16-19). Even the tree of life is now kept from man, though whether it was God's intention that man should eat of it in the Garden of Paradise is not definitely stated.[1]

---

[1] Thus it is not at all clear whether the Yahwist writer intended to infer that man was created to live without death. His thought is more on the current state of man's life than on its original possibilities. Later theology, of course, assumed the direct relation of sin and physical death as being involved: e.g. I Cor. 15.21-22.

The reason for the Divine sentence on man's life is simply described in Gen. 3 as his self-assertion to do that which God told him not to do. In this willed act of disobedience man has obtained a knowledge of good and evil (i.e., all knowledge, Divine knowledge) which God did not want him to have for his own good. In active disobedience to God man becomes conscious of the evil use to which the good can be put; and unhealthy sexual self-consciousness as something abnormal is given as an example. In his disobedient act man used his mind to rationalize what he was doing, so that the act at first did not appear as an evil. Its real nature became apparent only when he was confronted with God's judgment, faced with which, however, he failed to 'come clean' but laid the blame on his tempter, thus evading any acceptance of responsibility. Why should man have been created to act in this typical way? The story gives no answer; this is simply the way man is. It is not God's intention that he be so; but he uses his will and his mind to act against God, and then because of pride cannot clear his guilt before God by a straightforward confession and repentance. According to this story the fundamental sin of all mankind is the wilful disobedience of God which is compounded through fear and pride when faced with the penalty. As a result, there exists a personal estrangement between man and God. Yet this does not mean complete separation from God; it means rather a separation from Paradise and a relationship with God as an unrepentant, or at best only partially repentant, sinner.

Deprived of Paradise man evolves his civilization, not with attention to God's governing will, but simply without reference to it. The Yahwist writer uses his traditions in such a way as to show with each stage of civilization its spiritual problem; and matters become increasingly worse with the growth of social complexity. Thus the culmination of the narrative is the growth and separation of the nations and languages, and this is associated with the story of the Tower of Babel, in which men are determined by their own efforts to make themselves a name by thrusting their structure to heaven itself (Chaps. 10-11).[1] We infer that the

[1] See further, the writer, *The Old Testament Against its Environment* (London and Chicago, 1950), pp. 52-3.

descendants of Noah responsible for this act should have known better inasmuch as the flood was adequate warning; but the peculiar thing, we infer, is that mankind learns so little from his history, as far as wilful self-assertion in independence of God is concerned. He thus contravenes the conditions of his creation, and finds himself in difficulty which he refuses to acknowledge as the judgment of God.

Such is the problem of all men and all human society with which the Bible begins. It is something assumed, not developed or argued. The narrative turns immediately to Abraham, in whose loins the elect nation resides. In the miscellany of stories concerning him and his successors in Genesis, one of the chief points to be observed is the spiritual problem of the elect. That problem is one of faith and trust which determine responsible human action before God. Abraham hears God's call and receives the Divine promises, but this is followed directly with the story of his lying about his wife in Egypt (Chap. 12). Sarah cannot take seriously the promise of a son. To help matters along according to a commonsense view of the situation she gives Hagar to Abraham by a custom permitted in contemporary law. Yet this promptly involves the family in a squabble which God himself has to resolve (Chap. 16). Both Abraham and Sarah have received and believed the promises of God. Their problem in these incidents is simply to trust God to fulfil them in and through every historical situation. Their sinful acts were not overt rebellions against God; in concrete situations they were in doubt and anxious. Failure to believe that God meant what he had promised led them continually to assert their own wills, and this plunged them deeper into trouble. This is the perennial problem of every good and faithful person; he wants to believe but in his anxiety cannot wait upon God.

This same problem of the elect is illustrated again and again in the Biblical story. The Israelites believed that God had saved them from Egypt; yet in the wilderness they murmured because they were anxious and desperate about their immediate situation. They were promised the land, but after spying it out were afraid they could not take it. In a later time the weak and vacillating Ahaz rejects the idea of a coalition with Syria and North Israel against Assyria, but he cannot let matters rest there. He must throw himself at the Assyrian in an appeal for aid; and this is the occasion for Isaiah's warning: 'If ye will not believe, surely ye shall not be established' (Isa. 7.9). A century earlier, Ahab desired to know the will of God before embarking on a campaign against Syrian encroachment in Transjordan. The prophets were consulted, but Ahab would listen only to those who said what he wanted to hear. Micaiah, who said the opposite, was put in prison (I Kings 22). In Jeremiah's day the rather pitiful Zedekiah came secretly to the prophet on at least two occasions after his government had confined the prophet to prison (Jer. 37-38). He seemed inwardly to believe that God was speaking by Jeremiah, but in the complex network of events and personalities he possessed neither the faith nor the will to act upon his knowledge of God's will in the current events.

In these illustrative incidents and in many others we have to do with people who are not disbelieving heathen. They are members of the elect community who believe in God and in God's active work. But the chief problem of the elect is that of a faith and trust in God, a complete and unqualified reliance upon God to do what he has promised in connection with previous or contemporary events. Fear and anxiety brought forth actions which were wrong, but their wrongness became clear only in the light of God's subsequent action, though it previously may have been inwardly suspected. Faith in this sense is thus the peculiar and central problem of the elect. It is not a belief in a series of doctrines concerning the existence of God; it is rather a trust in the promises of God and in his actual direction of all events so that the believer himself acts without self-assertion toward his own well-being and in complete reliance that God will make all things work together for good for those who accept his election. Consequently, the Apostle Paul in Galatians and Romans is able to show that what God primarily wants is our faith in him. By it alone are we justified, not by conformity to outward laws. Thus also the author of the Epistle to the Hebrews is able to describe the whole movement of Biblical history by means of the faith of the elect, though it was only complete with the coming of Christ and his Church (Heb. 11). In other religions this type of faith is really unknown. Yet in the Bible it is the primary response which the God of history desires of those whom he calls. It is the chief problem in the life of the elect because in the events of history we become frightened and anxious. The besetting sin of the elect is not primarily a legal matter, and it is precisely this deeper dimension of the problem of faith and sin which propositional dogmatics has difficulty in stating. This is because it is the problem of walking with God in history, and it can only be made clear by narration.

IV

The problem of the elect, however, is further complicated by the fact that he does not exist in isolation before God, but that he has been placed by God within an elect community. This community exists and finds its true life in its responsible and living relationship with God as its Lord. The Pauline figure of the 'body' with the Lord as its head and the Johannine conception of the vine and its branches are not used in the old Testament, but they are excellent analogies for the whole Biblical conception of the meaning of community. In the Old Testament the picture most commonly in mind is that of the king and his subjects, though Hosea introduces still another analogy, that of a marriage relationship between husband and wife. In all four analogies (body, vine, kingdom, marriage) there is an inner and deep relationship between the two parties, any violation of which brings sickness or dissolution to the community. The Old Testament attempts to depict this relationship most commonly by means of legal or forensic terms, of which the chief is the conception of covenant. While the Ruler acts as King, Lord, Judge, Shepherd, and Saviour of his people, the latter as his subjects or servants are expected to keep his law. Righteousness is thus covenant-keeping; sin is the violation of covenant, and the grace of God is his remarkable *hesed*, that is his loyalty to his covenant-promises in the midst of covenant-breaking when there was absolutely no legal need for him to do so.

It is in this covenant context that the vocabulary of sin as rebellion, law-breaking, harlotry or whoredom arose. The great danger in such a conception is that the attention of the community

98

may be drawn more to the covenant ordinances than to their Giver. That this happened is clear. In Deuteronomy, for example, the very word 'covenant' is used as a name for the decalogue (Deut. 4.13, 23; cf. I Kings 8.21). To identify covenant with a law to be kept is so to emphasize the external, statutory nature of the compact as to push the spiritual bond and communion between God and people into the background. Deuteronomy itself preserves a proper balance between the two by its constant emphasis upon the extraordinary grace of God at the Exodus and in the wilderness. To these acts of God the only response is one of love. Our primary attachment to God should be one of a warm and complete devotion to him personally. If we possess this love, we will be completely and obediently loyal to him. Yet the tendency to identify covenant with the law of the covenant evidently was a reflection of what was happening among the people. Covenant as a purely juridical institution encouraged them to keep the outward forms of legal decency, while neglecting the deeper, inner relationship to God which alone made true community and true obedience.

Prophetic eschatology employs the covenant thought anew to depict the relationship with God which the future will bring. God will recreate the community with an 'everlasting covenant' (Isa. 55.3; 61.8; Jer. 32.40; Ezek. 37.26), a 'covenant of peace' (Isa. 54.10; Ezek. 34.25; 37.26), a 'new covenant' written upon the heart (Jer. 31.31-34). The servant of Second Isaiah is to be the mediator of the covenant for all people and as such the agent of their salvation (Isa. 42.6; 49.8). Here there is no longer a question about the nature of the covenant as an external, legal compact. It is based upon the pure grace of God which shall create in man a new heart and a new spirit to receive it. It is in this sense that the covenant conception is carried over into the Church. The Christian as a member of the new covenant in the blood of Jesus Christ becomes the heir of the election promises to Israel. Yet the basic conflict continued between the Apostle Paul and Judaism. It was concerned with the conception of the meaning of God's relation and revelation to his people as established in election and covenant. Judaism had identified covenant almost solely with the Mosaic law, with the result that the Apostle was no more able to use it in his struggle than were the prophets —except to oppose it.

The real problem of the elect community, like that of the elect individual within it, was one of faith to believe and to follow without question the leading of God in every situation. Consequently, the Biblical narrative describes the people's struggle for security and well-being in history, together with God's response to their acts. Disregarding God, they assert themselves in a groping fashion along several different paths at the same time, many of which were contradictory. Israel demanded and received a king, in imitation of the pagans, to provide justice and to fight their battles. An elaborate attempt was made to theologize the nature of the office and to fit it into the national eschatology. Yet Hosea at the beginning of the Assyrian crisis could say in God's name: 'Where now is thy king that he may save thee in all thy cities, and thy judges, of whom thou didst say: "Give me a king and princes"?' (Hos. 13.10). And Isaiah could present Ahaz with the proclamation of God's own Immanuel (Isa. 7.14). The priests called the people to rally around the Temple. This was the sign and seal of the presence of God in the midst of the community. Their call to the Temple was deceptively sincere, and it is not unlike the current summons to Christians to rally to the Church that civilization may be saved. Yet both Jeremiah and Jesus foresaw God's destruction of the Temple because it was used as almost a magical device, a substitute for true security which resides in God alone.[1]

In Israel between the tenth and seventh centuries there came the inevitable growth in social complexity with the result that the older simple order of equality before God in the covenant was disrupted. Even when the law was formally kept, how could one control the violation of its spirit in the midst of mounting social and economic pressures which any law has difficulty in containing? In addition, the growing centres of economic power made the temptation for exploitation and corruption irresistible. Yet the dependence of the government upon these centres of power was inevitably real because of the grave need for stability and increas-

[1] Jer. 7 and 26; Matt. 12.6; 24.2; 26.61. See Walther Eichrodt, *Theology Today*, Vol. VII (1950), pp. 15-25.

ing taxation. It is precisely the powerful who shower the greatest gifts both upon the throne and the sanctuary. We have to live; we want to live well; the government must have firm support among the classes who possess the financial resources; the army must be maintained; the sanctuaries should prosper; etc. In such a situation faith in God is difficult to make relevant, because the people live constantly amidst compromise. Thus faith and the common life become separated pursuits. Yet the prophets were far more radical in their proclamation of God's will without compromise. The advance of civilization apart from faith and by compromise is sin, a violation of covenant, and the disruption of community. Consequently, every social pressure available from people, priests and government was employed to stifle prophecy, or at least to turn it into more agreeable channels. This meant that the prophets were asked not to prophesy 'right things' but 'smooth things' which were 'deceits' (Isa. 30.10). To Jeremiah it was 'a wonderful and horrible thing' that both prophets and priests were false to their calling and that the 'people love to have it so; but what will ye do in the end thereof?' (Jer. 5.30-31). The problem of distinguishing the true from the false prophet thus became acute, and the people in their life of compromise did not possess the critical acumen which the covenant faith with its belief in God's jealousy was capable of providing. The correct interpretation of the will and intention of God in the current crises could be heard only in dim and blurred sounds (cf. Jer. 23; 28; Ezek. 13).

Furthermore, the imperialism of the reigning power in Mesopotamia threw both people and government into a flurry of political activity, flitting about, as Hosea put it, like a silly dove from this power to that (Hos. 6.11), hiring lovers and being swallowed up among the nations. Yet many believed that security could be found in the proper political alliances and defensive measures. To the prophets this was a manifest rebellion against God, because Israel was not called to be another nation among nations; and to act as though she were was a complete rejection of faith in God's Lordship over all events. As Isaiah put it, the people's true strength and security, which they rejected, was 'in returning and rest', 'in quietness and in confidence'; but they have chosen to flee upon horses swiftly, so flee they shall and the pursuit shall be equally swift (Isa. 30.15-16). Their preparations for security are comparable to a man trying to stretch himself in a bed too short for him, and to wrap himself in a covering that is too narrow (Isa. 28.20). The politicians believed that they had bought off destruction by their political covenants, but it is an attempt to set a refuge in lies and to hide in falsehood (Isa. 28.14-15).

Furthermore, when Israel and Judah were forced to knuckle under the Assyrian power, the temptation was strong to lessen the religious tension by compromise with the overlord's polytheism. Manasseh, we are told for example, introduced the worship of the heavenly bodies, the host of heaven, into the courts of the Temple along with other pagan rites (II Kings 21.5). After all, Yahweh possessed and presided over a heavenly court of divine beings (or angels); it would appear to be no radical a matter to identify some of these beings and offer them worship as did the surrounding pagans. In this way some of the 'uncultured' intolerance and exclusivism of Israel's faith might be lessened and life with pagans made more tolerable. Yet to the prophets no divided loyalty between God and the gods could survive; this tolerant compromise was an utterly faithless response to the God who had so graciously brought the nation into being, revealed in the wilderness the simplicity of his demands in worship and throughout the subsequent history had been so constant in revealing by acts and prophets his will and warning.[1]

V

Finally, we may mention still another attempt to get on in the world with safety and at least some degree of equanimity. This was the pursuit of what was called 'wisdom'. The wise men were evidently a special class in the community, as distinct from priests and prophets, whose function was to give practical advice on the proper way of life (Jer. 18.18; Ezek. 7.26). They came under the

[1] For the meaning of this point of view toward compromise for the conception of Biblical monotheism, see further the writer, *The Old Testament Against its Environment*, pp. 30-41. To the Protestant, of course, the reverence accorded in some sections of the Church to the saints, angels and the Virgin Mary ought to be brought under the same prophetic condemnation.

same prophetic condemnation as the priests and popular prophets.
Nevertheless, they were considered an important source of knowledge by the people and three of their books, Proverbs, Job and
Ecclesiastes, were retained in the canon. Their teaching as
typified in Proverbs is chiefly practical, prudential, and utilitarian,
much of it beautifully phrased and easily quoted. The primary
source of their insight in such teaching was keen observation,
experience and common sense. Yet like many sermons on character education, they represent for the most part the type of thing
which any man of good will can say, regardless of theological
affiliation. Consequently, it should be no surprise to observe that
the wisdom type of interest and of epigram existed in Egypt and
in Canaan also, and that many of Israel's proverbs were undoubtedly borrowed from international collections. Perhaps this is
fortunate, because Proverbs indicates that a prudential, commonsense ethic was not excluded from Biblical faith, though it does
raise a severe problem when confronted with the more radical
ethic elsewhere in both the Old and New Testaments, wherein
shrewd calculation is largely excluded, or at any rate secondary.

In any attempt to outline a discussion of Biblical faith it is the
wisdom literature which offers the chief difficulty because it does
not fit into the type of faith exhibited in the historical and prophetic literatures. In it there is no explicit reference to or development of the doctrine of history, election or covenant. Yet it
should be emphasized more strongly than heretofore that the
theological base of international wisdom was radically shifted
when it was brought into Israel. The good and the bad are not
those who maintain or disrupt the harmonious integration of
society, as in Egypt.[1] They are rather the righteous or upright
and the wicked or the foolish. This means that a standard of
evaluation is used which can only be the law of Yahweh; that is,
the peculiarly Israelite understanding of what constitutes good
and evil. The motto of the wisdom movement in Israel was 'the
fear of Yahweh', which is the beginning of knowledge and wisdom (Prov. 1.7; 9.10). Thus Yahweh is the true source of wisdom
(cf. Job. 28) and the author of prudential morality. It is he who
rewards the righteous and punishes the wicked.

[1] Cf. H. Frankfort, *Ancient Egyptian Religion* (New York, 1948), Chap. 3.

Nevertheless, while the wisdom teachers possessed an understanding of the individual, they lacked the peculiarly Israelite doctrine of society. Their extremely individualized doctrine of Divine reward and punishment furnished the setting for an inevitable theological controversy. The Book of Job was written to affirm a mystery in much human suffering which this doctrine cannot explain. The prophetic teaching concerning the judgment of God upon human sin is not necessarily rejected by the author. The objection is rather to the subtle inversion of that doctrine, wherein the presence of individual suffering is regarded as a proof of God's judgment upon individual sin. There is a deeper dimension in life than this; in the plan of God there is a mystery in his dealing with men which must be humbly accepted without loss of faith in his providence.

Ecclesiastes, on the other hand, represents a development in another direction toward a denial of the whole belief in individual rewards and punishments in this life or hereafter. God's moral government of the world, if it exists at all, is beyond our comprehension. The ordinary pursuits of men are vanity. God's administration of the world cannot be understood by man, for whether one is good or evil, death is the great leveller in which both perish (e.g. Eccl. 8.16-9.6). Yet wisdom is indeed better than folly, and the proper life is one which enjoys the simple pleasures here and now in the fear of God. The portion which God has given every man is the enjoyment of eating, drinking and labour, while avoiding self-assertive folly.

The difficulty of the wisdom movement was that its theological base and interest were too narrowly fixed; and in this respect Proverbs remains near the pagan source of wisdom in which society and the Divine work in history played no real role. In the canon of Scripture, Proverbs has the important function of supplying an explanation of the meaning of the law for individual life.[1] But to survive as a living force in Judaism and Christianity the wisdom movement had to undergo a more thorough acclimation to the doctrines of election and covenant. This was done, on the one hand, in the apocryphal Wisdom of

---

[1] See further H. Wheeler Robinson, *Inspiration and Revelation in the Old Testament* (Oxford, 1946), Chaps. XVIII-XX.

Solomon wherein eschatology is employed to overcome the difficulties of the writer of Ecclesiastes. On the other hand, the Book of Ecclesiasticus exalts Mosaic law, the study of which is actually the source of wisdom, and, therefore, is of universal validity.[1] Hence the problems presented by Job and Ecclesiastes failed to make any real dent on the religious life of the continuing community.

What specific advice the wise men gave to the Judean community in the time of Jeremiah and Ezekiel we do not know. Certainly these prophets were unimpressed with the counsel of the wise, for the latter were warned not to glory in their wisdom any more than the rich man should glory in his wealth, because the only true knowledge is the knowledge of God who exercises *hesed* (covenant-loyalty), justice and righteousness in the earth (Jer. 9.23-24). Furthermore, the days are at hand when their counsel will perish along with the false word of the popular prophets and the law of priests (Chap. 18.18).[2]

VI

In a situation such as that in which Israel found herself in the world of her day, how were the elect to know their sin? They were so deeply involved in self-assertive accommodation that they were simply unaware of the real nature of their problem. Consequently, they could not understand God's true prophets, and, at best, only partially believe them. The prophetic proclamation of God's will, demand and intention in the history of the time was so absolute that even responsible statesmen and citizens probably received it then as now as irrelevant and irresponsible. We must live in this world as it is, they may well have thought, and God will not help those who do not help themselves. This is the perennial dilemma of the elect and the embarrassment of the man of faith who enters political life. Yet the prophets were not legislators; their mission was completed with their proclamation.

[1] See further J. Coert Rylaarsdam, *Revelation in Jewish Wisdom Literature* (Chicago. 1946), pp. 27-46.
[2] Ezekiel 18 with its extreme individualistic emphasis may well have been influenced by the wisdom movement's teaching of the individual's rewards and punishments in this life. It is an extremely tendential chapter, written against a current proverb which excused that present generation from any responsibility in the crisis of the time.

And the strange fact is that subsequent events proved the correctness of that proclamation. Furthermore, those who survived the
catastrophes of the two kingdoms were finally convinced of their
corporate sin. It was not the law alone but the judgment involved
in the historical acts of God as proclaimed by the prophets which
brought the full realization of their true state. Yet since God
could not be defeated in his historical purpose, the men of faith
could not despair. Thus Jeremiah could pray fervently and
confidently: 'Though our iniquities testify against us, work thou
for thy name's sake, O Lord' (Chap. 14.7).

Much additional material could be added concerning the Biblical understanding of man and society, both from the Old Testament and from the New. The latter especially has received little
discussion in this chapter. Yet the purpose of this discussion is
not complete analysis, but a sampling of the material in order to
indicate its nature. The Biblical concentration on history as the
acts of God involves also the story of what man has done. As
the Biblical 'doctrine' of God is primarily a recital of what he has
done together with the inferences drawn from it, so also is the
'doctrine' of man. But 'doctrine' in this sense has its own special
and peculiar character, which allows for flexibility and variety in
modes of expression and insight and which necessitates the use
of narration to depict what is involved.

CHAPTER FIVE

FROM RECITAL TO MODERN THEOLOGY

IN the Christian Church the subject matter of revelation has frequently been conceived as infallible doctrine, which in turn is thought of as a series of propositions which can be supported by the citation of numerous proof-texts from the Bible. In this sense the Bible has been used as a source of revealed doctrine. It is clear, however, that the Bible does not present us with doctrine of this type, and the attempt to make it do so is to misuse it. In its pages we are not confronted first of all with a series of rational, infallible, theological abstractions, but with the person of the living God and of his Son, our Lord, Jesus Christ. We are also confronted with the activity of men in whom we see ourselves, so that the distance between the Biblical generations and our generation is bridged and we become participants in the original history in order to participate rightly in our own. For what is history but the interacting 'Challenge-and-response' movement between God and man which God is directing to his own good? To speak of it as a 'dialogue' between God and man is to employ a limited metaphor which confines it to speech and communication. Yet the primary means by which God communicates with man is by his acts, which are the events of history. These events need interpretation, it is true, and God provides it in his Word by chosen heralds or messengers. But the focus of attention is not upon the Word of God in and for itself so that it can be frozen, so to speak, within a system of dogmatic propositions. The Word leads us, not *away from* history, but *to* history and to responsible participation *within* history. It is the accompaniment of history. The Bible thus is not primarily the Word of God, but the record of the Acts of God, together with the human response thereto.

The subject matter of both Biblical and dogmatic theology, therefore, is the confessional recital of the unique events of Biblical history, together with the inferences and interpretations which the Word in Biblical faith by historian, prophet, psalmist, apostle and evangelist drew from them or associated with them. When this conception of the subject matter of theology is kept central, then we are delivered from the temptation to impose a static uniformity or unity upon the Bible, or, for that matter, on the theology of the Church. The problem of the modern scholar regarding the relation between Biblical theology and the history of Biblical religion no longer seems so acute and insoluble. Variety, change, even disagreement and discrepancy are to be expected within the Bible, if we take this viewpoint seriously. Yet the variety is never of such a nature as to constitute a totally different series of theologies, because the central and especial concern with the meaning of historical events and of life within history holds the whole together, or in the end, as in the case of the wisdom literature, subsumes all within itself.

But, it may be objected, how do we get from recital to the modern Church and the modern world? We live in an age which needs and demands something more than a series of interpreted stories. Our age is more Hellenic than Hebraic. The Christian Church must of necessity present the faith in a logical, coherent, reasoning and reasonable form. This is certainly true, and for my part I have never been stimulated by the attempts to set mind and faith over against one another in such a way as to create a rational paradox which needs to be resolved by the argumentative assertion of one over against the other. Biblical psychology with its unitary view of man would appear to be a valid corrective to such simple distortion. Consequently, it must be maintained that both Christian philosophy and 'systematic' theology have the exceedingly important function of analysing and interpreting the faith in its many aspects and of making its relevance to modern man apparent.

Theology may perhaps be defined as the discipline by which the Church, carefully and with full knowledge of the risk, translates Biblical faith into the non-Biblical language of another age. It is an extension of the Bible into the non-Biblical world. It is true theology only if it is under the same mandate as was Biblical man; the translation will fail unless it is itself controlled by that authority which produced the Bible, God himself through the Holy Spirit. The Bible is the record of the acts of God, but it remains nothing more than a record when theology forsakes the task for which it exists. In so far as Protestantism has avoided

both bibliolatry and mysticism, it has done so by insisting
that the truth comes into life when the Bible and the Holy
Spirit express their unity in the life of faith and the life of the
mind.

Yet both Christian theology and philosophy must be under the
constant restraint of the Biblical presentation of the faith. Their
independent existence must be qualified by their dependence
upon that without which they would not be. A tension will
always exist between the Bible and our attempts to communicate
its faith in rational language at a given historical period. The
faith is greater than our attempts to express it and deeper than
any one individual can conceive in his historical finitude. Furthermore, the creeds of the Church which preserve our historical
continuity with the original revelation and discipline our tendencies toward paganism are not in themselves a substitute for the
Bible. They are not sacrosanct in the sense that they bear the
same authority as the Bible itself. The faith of the Church must
constantly be reformed and illumined on the basis of fresh study
of the Bible. A relatively static authoritarianism, of the Roman
Catholic, Fundamentalist or any other type, so confuses the
authority of the Church and its creeds with the authority of
Biblical faith that the tension which God places between himself
and our human understanding is removed. Certainly the removal
of this tension is the first step in opening the doors of the Church
to idolatry.

Nevertheless, when this has been said, the suspicion still
remains that the systematic presentation of abstract dogma cannot
and should not be the primary teaching method of the Church.
In part this is because propositional dogmatics lacks the colour,
the flexibility, the movement of the Bible and because it attempts
to freeze into definite, prosaic, rationality that which was never
intended by the Bible so to be frozen and which by its very nature
cannot be so construed. For example, a Confession of Faith for
which I have great respect is that of my own communion (Presbyterian). A portion of its chapter on God reads as follows:

I. There is but one only living and true God, who is infinite
in being and perfection, a most pure spirit, invisible, without
body, parts, or passions, immutable, immense, eternal, incom-

prehensible, almighty, most wise, most holy, most free, most absolute, working all things according to the counsel of his own immutable and most righteous will, for his own glory; most loving, gracious, merciful, long-suffering, abundant in goodness and truth, forgiving iniquity, transgression, and sin; the rewarder of them that diligently seek him; and withal most just and terrible in his judgments, hating all sin, and who will by no means clear the guilty.

II. God hath all life, glory, goodness, blessedness, in and of himself; and is alone in and unto himself all-sufficient, not standing in need of any creatures which he hath made, nor deriving any glory from them, but only manifesting his own glory in, by, unto, and upon them: he is the alone fountain of all being, of whom, through whom, and to whom are all things; and hath most sovereign dominion over them, to do by them, for them, and upon them, whatsoever himself pleaseth. In his sight all things are open and manifest; his knowledge is infinite, infallible, and independent upon the creature, so as nothing is to him contingent or uncertain. He is most holy in all his counsels, in all his works, and in all his commands. To him is due from angels and men, and every other creature, whatsoever worship, service, or obedience, he is pleased to require of them.

By its very cold, abstract and tight nature such a definition of God somehow separates us from his living, active and warm Presence which we come to know by contemplation of what he has done and by seeing ourselves as the recipients of his gracious work. What is here said may all be true and very important, and yet it does not quite introduce us to the Biblical God. The Church's liturgy, its hymns and prayers, have preserved much more of the active, vivid, existential nature of the Biblical knowledge of God. In short, this definition gives the impression of being dull and pompous; the Biblical presentation by contrast is interesting, *unpretentious*, simple, alive. Is this accidental, or does our dull abstractness betray our separation from Biblical faith, in which the nature of God is taught us by the narration of what he has done? Is there not always the danger of focussing attention by abstraction upon the being of God in and for himself and thus separating ourselves from the Bible with its serious attention to history in which God alone is known? If so, then the Church's theology must always beware of the scholastic tendency to become unhistorical. This perhaps is the primary lesson and the primary warning which the Bible imposes upon the Church's theologians.[1]

II

The problem remains, however, as to how we are to outline and present Biblical theology. Its primary nature as recital of God's acts in history prevents us from using the rubrics of systematic theology in the customary static and abstract form: i.e., the doctrine of God, the doctrine of man, the doctrine of sin, the doctrine of redemption, the doctrine of Christ, the doctrine of the Church, etc. In the Bible these 'doctrines' are so interrelated in a historical context that they cannot be separated and examined entirely as independent objects of reflection.

Furthermore, it must be said that as Christians we are committed to the Bible as a whole, not to one of the Testaments alone. We must be dissatisfied, therefore, with the current separation of the Bible into compartments, with the various books on New Testament theology and Old Testament theology which leave it up to the reader to put the whole together, and with the present situation in our theological schools in which the Biblical teachers are separated into Old and New Testament departments. This is one skeleton in the closet of the Church which needs more dusting than it has received. At the moment almost every work on any phase of Biblical faith (including this one) is marred in some measure by this compartmentalizing of the Church's scholarship, so that insufficient attention has been given to the manner in which the whole Bible becomes in Christ the source of the Church's proclamation. New Testament scholars have presumed to depict a New Testament theology which in fact does not exist in isolated independence since to every New Testament writer the 'scrip-

---

[1] It should be said, of course, that the Westminster definition, quoted above, came out of the period of Protestant scholasticism. It is very improbable that the Reformers would ever have constructed such a statement.

tures' are not what they themselves are writing but actually the literature relating to the old covenant. For a New Testament scholar of the Church to become more of a specialist in Judaism and Hellenism than he is of the Old Testament is thus surely rather incongruous. Old Testament scholars, on the other hand, have been much more concerned with the establishment of themselves and their discipline among orientalists than they have among Christians in the Church (not, of course, that all orientalists are pagans!). Yet we who are called by the Church to specialize in and to teach the Old Testament cannot carry on our work as though Jesus Christ had not come or as though the New Testament were irrelevant to our work with the Old. A book such as that of I. G. Matthews', *The Religious Pilgrimage of Israel* (New York and London, 1947), in which the culmination of this pilgrimage is seen in Judaism, while the New Testament is dismissed with one brief paragraph on the Nazarenes, is surely an extreme example of Christian anachronism.[1] In such a situation it is difficult to see how the Church is to avoid the recurring tendencies toward a Marcionite understanding of the Bible.

In attempting to present Biblical theology as a whole according to the viewpoint here presented, considerable variation in method of treatment is conceivable. It is improbable that any one person in one particular historical situation can present a treatment that is entirely satisfactory. Yet certain things are clear.

(1) It is important that we begin with the Gospel of which we are heirs and which in the Church we proclaim. This is the Biblical *kerygma* as briefly outlined in Chapter III above. We thus begin as Christians with the New Testament, with its proclamation of Christ, his life, death and resurrection, his present Lordship over the Church of which we are members by faith, called to be his witnesses while awaiting his second advent and the fulfilment of history. Thence we reach back into the Old Testament in order to see what its proclamation

[handwritten margin note: Begin with N.T. kerygma then → O.T.]

---

[1] It is perhaps unfair to single out this one book for mention when all of us are culpable to a greater or lesser degree. A further example of our predicament is that it is difficult to find a leading graduate school in the world where a student can profitably specialize in Biblical theology; he must become either an Old Testament scholar (and thus something of an orientalist) or a New Testament scholar (and thus with some expert knowledge of Judaism and Hellenism, but not necessarily of the Old Testament)!

of God's saving acts was, and thus to understand what Christ means as the culminating event in a special redemptive history.

At this point we may pause to reflect on the significance of this recital, its particular view of history, its astonishing and radical difference from the world's religions, its demand for participation and decision, its relation to the Word and teaching of the Bible. Thereafter, however, we must begin the treatment of the Biblical inferences which were drawn from what God has done; and this, it seems to me, must be done historically. One of the central Biblical assumptions is God's mediate means of working in history; it is his choice of a people, a *qahal* or *ekklesia*, through whom he has purposed to effect his plan in history. In other words, as stated in Chapter II, the primary Biblical inference from the record of what God has done is his election of Israel of which we are heirs in the Church. Our treatment of this would include some investigation of how the conception arose, what was meant by it and what was not, the purpose and history of it. It is only after this 'doctrine' of election has been described as the primary act of God's grace that we should begin the treatment of the covenant. Unless we keep grace and election first, covenant may appear as a juridical and forensic arrangement; thus the central emphasis of the Bible may be betrayed, as happened, for example, in Judaism and in the Federal Theology of Protestantism. Gospel as known from the *kerygma* precedes the Divine requirement in the law of the Covenant, and it is by our faith that we are ultimately justified, not by our good deeds in obedience to the law. To be sure the whole Bible does not speak to this point with a completely unanimous voice, and the variations of emphasis must be described. Yet there can scarcely be any doubt that on this point the Apostle Paul has portrayed correctly the deepest insight of the Old Testament (cf. Chapter IV above).

The setting of the covenant was an event, God's formation of the nation at Sinai-Horeb and the giving of the law. It was based on a political anthropomorphism in which God appeared as 'Lord' and 'King', and his people as his subjects or 'servants', who were called upon 'to love', 'to hearken to' and 'to obey' the ruler. Righteousness was *ḥesed* or covenant-loyalty and 'truth' (*'emeth*) was firm fidelity to the Ruler's will. God himself is the

God of *ḥesed* and *'emeth* because of his gracious loyalty to his promises, and the 'grace and truth' of Jesus Christ (John 1.14) are not abstract virtues but the active *ḥesed* and *'emeth*, rooted in the covenant conception. Both Israel and the Church are God's 'Kingdom' and prefigure the universal 'Kingdom' which God is establishing. Moreover, covenant furnished the understanding of community among the redeemed people; it was the revealed order of society which prefigured the universal order, yet to be consummated by God, and which illuminated the actual state of existing societies.

This treatment of the covenant might then be followed by a treatment of the Biblical conception of the inheritance, derived from God's gift of the land in the conquest, and by the conception and problem of government, including human kingship, the kingship of Christ, the relation of the elect to the government of foreign powers in both the Old and the New Testaments, the role of prophecy in God's governing of the elect, etc.

(2) At this point, in order to complete the survey of inferences drawn from the recital of God's acts, we might well turn to the subject of God and his creation. It should be introduced after the treatment of election and covenant, so it seems to me, because the particular Biblical view of nature and man as God's creation are only apparent to those who know themselves to be redeemed and who proclaim what God has done. This is further supported by the form criticism of the Old Testament, from which it is clear that the oldest and primary confessions of faith did not contain reference to God's creative acts, and as well by the earliest Christian confessions which were Christological, not Trinitarian. The treatment of God's creative activity would involve his relation to nature and the conception of nature, which would also bring up the subject of God and the gods of nature, the conception of man, the means by which God exercises his sovereignty over the world, the manner in which he reveals himself in the world, etc. Here would be included, perhaps, a treatment of the so-called 'attributes' of God, which are not static qualities as frequently treated, but inferences from the observed activity of God in his governance of the world.

(3) It would seem logical to treat in more detail in a third major

114

section the life of man and of his society on earth, together with the work and purpose of God in respect to it. This would raise the questions of the creature's revolt, his sin and its consequences, death as alienation or separation from God, the means man evolves for achieving his security in history,[1] the historical judgments of God on human society, man's subjection to the power of Satan (in the New Testament), etc. This would properly be followed by a more detailed treatment than was necessary in the first section, of Biblical eschatology, of the redemptive work of God, of the meaning of the atoning work of Christ, of the consummation of God's kingdom, and of the means of entrance into it (including the subjects relating to the Second Coming, the final judgment, and resurrection).

(4) The above outline thus far has left out a number of subjects, the chief of which are those relating to the worship of God and the service of God. Properly they would belong in the first section under God's election of the redeemed community and of the manner in which he has bound it to himself and in which he governs it. Yet in order not to interrupt that discussion too much, it might be well to include a detailed treatment of the means and manner of worship (its basis, its forms and places) and of the law for the common life in a final section, wherein the focus of attention is upon the temporal means by which God is now to be served and worshipped.

It cannot be argued that the above outline is the only possible one. It is here given solely as an example of how the data of Biblical faith may be treated in such a way as to preserve its history-centred (or as the Germans call it, *heilsgeschichtlich*) nature. We are thus kept nearer both to history and to the recital of history by faith than is possible by the systematic methodology which actually tends to separate what is felt to be the *intellectual* content both from the faith and from its rootage in history. It is a very popular notion that theology deals with a religion's intellectual content, as though there were possible a divorce between theology and religion, between reason and faith, between intellectual knowledge and empirical or existential experience. If one

---

[1] In any outline of Biblical theology, the proper place to treat the wisdom literature is something of a problem. As indicated in Chapter IV, however, I should be inclined to place it here.

accepts a Biblical view of the unitary nature of man, such a definition of theology becomes impossible because one cannot understand how a religion can be divided up into compartments this way. Life, reason, faith are a part of one whole, and theology must deal with and attempt to communicate that whole. Biblical theology cannot be completely unsystematic—indeed it must constantly and critically observe its own discrepancies and paradoxes—but it is not primarily concerned with an abstract 'system of thought'. It is rather a reflective discipline which seeks to portray the peculiar Biblical concern with man's involvement in a God-directed history and with God's activity relative to man's historical problem, need and hope.

An obvious criticism to be levelled at the above attempt to outline a Biblical theology is simply that it again attempts to systematize the unsystematizable. This is true. It is also true that the needs of the Church demand that we make such an attempt in full knowledge that it will be neither final nor sacrosanct. It will be a temporal effort which speaks to its own generation and situation; it cannot be considered as a work of objective 'science' which will be eternally valid. The real issue, however, is whether a Biblical theology can be written by the use of categories drawn from the Bible itself, instead of from propositional dogmatics, and whether the work can be done in a reflective manner without an emphasis upon dogmatic and over simple systematization. In other words, the fundamental requirement of a Biblical theology is that the historical movement and interaction of the Bible be retained while the faith is being set forth in summary statements true to its own nature.

III

For the modern Church, however, a crucial problem exists as to what should be done with the Biblical theology of recital. The Bible is the record of God's acts of wrath, love and salvation in a certain specific history which is set within the framework of all history and presents to all history the hope and certainty of its redemption. The Biblical perspective of time thus carries back before Abraham to the creation. It leads forward to the death and resurrection of Jesus Christ as its mid-point, and beyond that to the end of present history and the dawn of eternity. This eternity is not a timeless existence which men enter through the dissociation of soul from body by a natural process of transmutation. Death is taken much more seriously as the end of life, the annihilation of the 'soul' (*nephesh*). Eternity is the redemption of the present time and its extension. It is time stretched out, and one enters it by a miracle of God's creation, the resurrection of the body.[1]

In the presentation of this view it is true that the Bible takes historical facts seriously, but in doing so reaches back before history to prehistory and creation. Furthermore, in dealing with historical data it does so with an unprovable assumption that God is the central actor in history, and it considers as historical events matters which to the modern mind seem simply to be human ideas or human faith projected into history. Thus the covenant at Sinai is clearly a human event, but is it a Divine act in history? The deliverance of Israel from Egyptian slavery at the time of Moses is a fact, but is it also a historical fact that God had chosen Israel for his special possession? The death of Jesus on a cross is certainly an event in history, but is his resurrection and exaltation to God's right hand also a definite and actual event? We today insist that facts should be verifiable, but in Biblical history the primary meaning seen in events, and many matters which are considered events, are not verifiable. They are a projection of faith into facts which is then considered as the revelation of the true meaning of the facts. The pagan's suspicion and rejection of the Bible is thus understandable. A new Russian dictionary of 20,000 'foreign' (non-Russian) words and phrases, recently published by the Soviet State Publishing House, defines 'religion' as 'a fantastic faith in Gods, angels and spirits . . . a faith without any scientific foundations . . . supported and maintained by the reactionary circles . . . for the subjugation of the working people'. The Bible is defined as 'a collection of fantastic legends without any scientific support . . . full of dark hints, historical mistakes and contradictions'.[2]

---

[1] See especially Oscar Cullmann, *Christ and Time* (tr. by Floyd V. Filson; Philadelphia, 1950 and London, 1951).

[2] *Christianity and Crisis*, Vol. XI, No. 1 (Feb. 5, 1951), p. 7.

Many theologians today are attempting to deal with this problem of the Bible by a revival of the term 'myth'. They assume that myth and history are so interwoven in the Bible that the whole may be said to possess a mythical character.[1] One of two attitudes is taken with regard to the Biblical mythology.

(1) The first is to regard myth as something essentially untrue and foreign to the modern mind. Consequently, if the Biblical *kerygma* is to be understood and accepted by modern man, it must be demythologized. This is the position of the German New Testament scholar, Rudolf Bultmann, whose essay on 'New Testament and Mythology: The Problem of the De-mythologizing of the New Testament Proclamation' has inaugurated a major theological discussion in Europe.[2]

(2) The second and more common theological solution is to say that reason and science in dealing with historical facts can only observe the sequence and causality in empirical data, and thus tend toward a mechanistic interpretation of reality. They cannot deal with the ultimate questions of the organic unity of all reality, of the dimension of depth in human experience, of beginning and ending, and of the 'beyond' which transcends experience. The only way the human mind has to deal with these deeper meanings in and beyond present experience is to draw upon intuition and imagination and present pictures, use metaphors, and tell stories. Biblical mythology, for example that concerned with Satan, thus does not give us something which is not true. It is the only means man has of dealing with and communicating ultimate truth. If we try to demythologize the Bible, we shall have nothing left but a group of historical facts which are scientifically verifiable to a greater or lesser degree.

As a result of this modern revival of the term 'myth', we have a

[1] E.g. H. and H. A. Frankfort in *The Intellectual Adventure of Ancient Man* (Chicago 1946), p. 373: 'With infinite *moral* courage the Hebrews worshipped an absolute God and accepted as the correlate of their faith the sacrifice of a harmonious existence. In transcending the Near Eastern myths of immanent godhead, they created ... the new myth of the will of God. It remained for the Greeks, with their peculiar *intellectual* courage, to discover a form of a speculative thought in which myth was entirely overcome.'

[2] See Hans Werner Bartsch, ed., *Kerygma und Mythos, Ein Theologisches Gespräch* (Hamburg, 1948). For an excellent review of the discussion in English, see Amos N. Wilder, 'Mythology and the New Testament', *Journal of Biblical Literature*, Vol. LXIX (1950), pp. 113-127.

peculiar situation in the Church. The Bible definitely and consciously repudiates the gods of the nations together with their mythology and their magic. To worship the God of Israel and the Father of Jesus Christ meant the discarding of nature myths of immanent gods and along with them virtually the whole magical cultus by which men integrated their lives with the life of nature which was the life of the gods. That which was held over or borrowed from paganism was either reinterpreted in the new setting or else the occasion for controversy.[1] Consequently, in the early Church 'science' and theology were allied against mythology. Today this alliance has become a problem. Either we keep it and demythologize Biblical theology, or else we discard it and ally theology and mythology against science. Such appears to be the dilemma with which the theologians are facing us.

The problem of demythologising the Bible is one which has been keenly felt only since the modern Enlightenment. The older liberal idealism of the nineteenth century believed that one could separate the kernel from the shell. That is, one could put aside the 'myth' of the will of an anthropomorphic God, of his choosing, judging and redeeming the people of Israel, of his raising Christ from the dead to be Lord of the Creation, ruling over the hosts of angels and men, judging the quick and the dead, as the shell which contains the valid kernel of ideals and ethical principles. In other words, we can simply discard the outworn world-view and historical interpretations and save that which is essential, namely the highest spiritual and ethical teachings. This, of course, is not only to demyth the Bible, but to de-historize it also. What is left are the best teachings, while the peculiar Biblical interest in history which so differentiates it from other religious literature is regarded as non-essential. In the words of Bultmann: 'The *kerygma* is here reduced to specific religious and ethical principles, and to a religiously motivated idealistic ethic. But therewith the truth of the *kerygma as kerygma is eliminated*, that is, as the message of the decisive operation of God in Christ. The great religious and ethical ideas are eternal, timeless truths . . . '[2]

[1] See further, the writer in *The Old Testament Against its Environment* (London and Chicago, 1950), especially Chap. III.

[2] *Kerygma und Mythos*, p. 26. Translation, except for the last sentence, is that of Amos N. Wilder, *op. cit.*, p. 123.

In recent years the problem of discarding the so-called mythology of the Bible has become much more difficult as the result of form criticism. It is now recognized that the central message of the Bible is a proclamation of the Divine action; and, if we discard that, we shall have nothing left which makes the Bible what it is. It is impossible to reduce the *kerygma* to a kernel consisting of a series of ethical teachings. The *kerygma* is itself the kernel to which the ethics are attached and from which they receive their meaning. The real question is to face quite frankly that which constitutes Biblical faith. It is not a social feeling primarily nor a sympathy for all life; it is first and foremost a confessional recital of the gracious and redemptive acts of God. If we cannot accept this as true, let us frankly say so; but we should not misinterpret the Bible by making timeless ethical and spiritual abstractions its core or kernel of truth.[1]

This is precisely the critique that Bultmann makes of the problem facing the older liberalism. He insists that it is not a question of selection or elimination in the Bible of what we do not like. We must take the *kerygma* as it stands and deal with it as a whole. When we do so, he believes, we discover that the Biblical myth is primarily concerned with man's situation and self-understanding; it 'is not so much cosmological as anthropological'.[2] The problem of man is his attempt to assert himself and to find his security solely in this world, which results in his bondage to the world and the exclusion of the possibilities which he has under God. The New Testament mythology connected with the conceptions of 'world', 'Satan', 'flesh', 'sin', 'death' can actually be translated, Bultmann believes, into terms which confront man with the real problem of his existence under God without the use of the mythology. Thus, the actual meaning of the Cross for us is not to believe in some mythical transaction between God and Christ in the past, but to share that Cross as our own. The resurrection cannot be described today as an actual historical

[1] A recent example of the demything of the Bible and the acceptance of the view that religion is simply the human quest for 'wholeness of life' (which wholeness is God), or vital exploration in the life of the spirit (in which it is possible that a personalized metaphysics should be replaced by a more functional or clinical approach to the life of persons), is that of Floyd H. Ross, *Journal of Bible and Religion*, Vol. XIX, No. 1 (Jan. 1951), pp. 3-5.

[2] Wilder, *op. cit.*, p. 115.

event; it is merely the pictorial assertion of the victory or the new life which comes to us when we 'die' to sin and are 'made alive' in Christ. It is the proclamation of the Cross as a saving-event. In this viewpoint, he asserts, we have demythologized the Bible without losing its essential context, which is God's action in Christ.

Before we raise any objections to Bultmann's view, we should frankly confess that he is simply putting into words something that even conservative sections of the American Church have long felt, though scarcely confessed openly. One need only read or listen to our weekly sermons to realize how completely we 'demythologize' the Gospel in our public proclamation of it. And we do so, either along the lines suggested by Bultmann or by means of the moralizing and spiritual-experience emphasis of the older liberalism.

One difficulty with the Bultmann view is the danger that it incurs of so individualizing Biblical faith that the sense of the meaningfulness of history is lost. There is surely something of urgent importance for us in the Bible that is prior to individual confrontation and self-understanding. That is the objective work of God in history which points forward to history's fulfilment. Without it what means does the Christian have of interpreting history, or of understanding the importance or significance of his call within it? Must we live solely by the individual hope of new life in God, or does not Biblical faith provide the ground for a more objective hope in the God who is the directing Lord of time and who will redeem the present by the creation of the new community in 'the new heavens and the new earth'? Without this faith in the Lord of history for what can we hope, other than the individual, almost self-centred, hope and trust in God's salvation?

Furthermore, if we do insist on the importance of this faith in the redeeming Lord of history, is it then possible to proclaim this faith without the use of those symbols, metaphors and stories which Bultmann calls 'mythology'? It is a question as to whether Bultmann himself has avoided that which he defines as 'myth'. Man does not 'meet' God as he meets another human being, nor can he 'hear' him with the same ears or 'obey' him with the same obedience. Is not the theme of existential confrontation in itself a form of 'myth', or at least necessarily expressed in metaphorical terms? As soon as we assert in any way the Lordship of God over history or God's revelation of himself in history, we have to use metaphors drawn from human experience, and we must describe the course of history in terms which to science are not verifiable and in that sense 'mythical'. It is no accident that the particular metaphors and historical analogies chosen by the Bible were used as a weapon against the current pagan myths. The selection was refined and its validity tested in the warfare against the gods. So rich and many-sided is the selection that it is to be doubted whether the Church can devise any significant improvements. On the contrary, the Church must preserve the original metaphors on which the faith rests, striving always to make clear just what is meant by them. Yet if this is done, then it will be difficult to avoid the use of what Bultmann considers to be 'mythology'.

The answer to Bultmann given by those who insist that we cannot demythologize the Bible is drawn along the above lines. The theologians who are employing the idea of myth as the ally of theology against science believe that Bultmann is not defining myth correctly. He thinks of it as that form of representation in which the otherworldly and the Divine appear as the worldly and the human in such a way as to be unreal, untrue and un-scientific. To him myth is that which contains no truth; it merely suggests man's problem and sense of his existence. It is a body of untenable conceptions which had meaning only for a particular age. This would seem to suggest that modern man can live on strictly rational and scientific fare alone. Yet this modern scientific age is precisely an age in which we have witnessed some of the most elaborate myth-making in history. We are surrounded by myths; we live and breath them. While the most spectacular is the mythology of communism, those in which we move are no less important. The spiritual life of the west has maintained itself by a supposedly scientific myth drawn from evolution, the idea of progress, which involves the unverifiable faith that man can be redeemed in history by gradual growth. Man, it is asserted, cannot live by science alone; he must also feed on poetry and mythology which point to the unity and meaning which transcend himself and his world. This 'dimension of depth' in existence points beyond the world because things, as they are, are not self-explanatory; it also indicates man's own internal awareness of his capacity to transcend himself and to assert that 'what is highest in spirit is also deepest in nature' (W. P. Montague). Thus Reinhold Niebuhr inverts the words of Santayana ('Poetry is religion which is no longer believed') and asserts: 'Religion is poetry which is believed'.[1] Consequently, those who seek to demythologize the Bible are attempting something which will convince no one, because science cannot give the final word about life. To be sure, 'religion had no right to insist on the scientific accuracy of its mythical heritage. From this position a retreat was necessary ... But there is a permanent as well as a primitive myth in every great mythical heritage. This deals with aspects of reality which are supra-scientific rather than pre-scientific. Modernistic religion has been so thin on the whole because it did not understand this distinction and thus sacrificed what is abiding with what is primitive in religious myth.'[2]

It is a question as to whether Bultmann, from this point of view, has also failed to make this distinction. In any event, there are many theologians today who are saying that the mythology of the Christian religion is not a mere time-conditioned pre-scientific error; it is the only means by which the truth of reality and the truth which explains experience can be proclaimed. *[true]* Furthermore, it is a saving truth which scientific preoccupation cannot handle. For Bultmann myth 'carries no truth. The myth of the Redeemer carries no truth. The myth of vicarious redemption carries no truth. The myth of world-judgment and a new age carries no truth.'[3] What then is the truth? Is it only that the individual can live a new life? Is there not a danger of so translating history and demything its interpretation that what is left is nothing but a religious psychology? In order to present the proclamation of the Lord of history we can only use the Biblical myths; there is no other way of communicating Biblical truth. Our danger is to assume that the myths convey, not

[1] 'The Truth in Myths', *The Nature of Religious Experience: Essays in Honor of Douglas Clyde Macintosh* (New York, 1937), p. 119.
[2] *Ibid.*, pp. 118-9.
[3] Wilder, *op. cit.*, p. 126.

merely truths of faith, but historical and scientific truths as well.

If one were forced to make a choice between the two positions outlined above, I, for my part, would align myself with the second. My difficulty with both, however, is, in the first instance, with their use of the term 'mythology'. What, after all, are both saying? Both believe over against the older liberal idealism that the central and characteristic thing in the Bible is the historical *kerygma* which cannot be discarded as though it were the shell surrounding the ethical teaching. Nevertheless, it is precisely this *kerygma* which is called 'mythology'. In other words, Biblical theology is indeed a theology of recital, but it is a projection of myth on history. The meaning of this is, of course, that belief in a theology of recital is a matter of faith, based upon one's knowledge of God and 'the dimension of depth' in human experience. Furthermore, influenced by the modern scientific outlook, the members of these two schools of thought insist that the confessional recital cannot be taken literally, as historical, but it must be viewed as a mytho-poetry which must be demythologized before it can be proclaimed today or else proclaimed openly as poetry, apprehended as much by the aesthetic sense as by the reason, but not treated as scientific truth. In one, myth is considered unnecessary for the modern man; in the other, it is seen with more truth as indispensable. But the real question to my mind is whether the term 'myth' is here used properly. When we use it in this way, are we not saying that Biblical faith *is* mythology?

What has happened, it seems to me, is the same thing that has happened to a number of other words in theology. Conceptions which originally in their own right had a certain definite and concrete meaning are taken from their proper context, given an extended meaning until their content is so watered that they can no longer be used in serious theological discussion. One example is the term 'mysticism'. Properly this describes a certain definite religious conception which arose in the religions of the east and which came into the Christian Church through Neo-Platonism. In the proper sense of the term the Bible is non-mystical; as frequently pointed out.[1] But in the modern day the term has come to be used for all religious intuition and experience; there-

---

[1] E.g., the writer in *The Challenge of Israel's Faith* (Chicago, 1944), Chap. III.

fore, for many, it is simply another name for 'religion'. When so used, it can no longer be employed in serious discussion because it lacks any clear definition in which clear-cut distinctions can be made. Christianity thus becomes allied with pagan mysticism against modern secular materialism. Perhaps there is a limited sense in which this is legitimate; but there is something about the Biblical point of view that reacts sharply against such 'fuzziness' and insists that clear-cut distinctions be made between Biblical faith and other faiths. As was suggested in Chapter One, Biblical faith is simply not mystical; it insists on an objectivity of faith which is not centred in internal, self-conscious and self-propelled experience.

We now have the same process going on with the term 'mythology'. It has its own proper meaning in the history of religions; it refers to the religious literature of polytheist religions which concentrated attention upon the life of nature and saw in it the life of the gods. Nature is alive for the polytheist; it is filled with powers to which man must integrate his own existence. When he spoke about the gods, he too told stories; but they are not set in history, nor primarily concerned with history. Actually, they combine a faith with imagination and pre-logical empirical observation in order to depict the working, the life of nature. The polytheist has 'the deep conviction of a fundamental and indelible *solidarity of life* that bridges over the multiplicity and variety of its single forms ... To mythical and religious feeling nature becomes one great society, the *society of life*. Man is not endowed with outstanding rank in this society. He is a part of it but he is in no respect higher than any other member. Life possesses the same religious dignity in its humblest and in its highest forms. Men and animals, animals and plants are all on the same level.'[1]

In this context the word 'mythology' makes definite sense. Yet modern theologians, with scarcely more than the most cursory regard for the word's proper meaning and with the most scanty attention to the theology of polytheism, now cheerfully 'steal' the word and say to the modern world: 'Christianity is mythology and to understand it we must demythologize it for you.' Or, they say: 'Christianity is mythology, but it is a true mythology, for

[1] Ernst Cassirer, *An Essay on Man* (New Haven, 1944), pp. 82-3.

you can only comprehend ultimate meaning in the world in terms of mythology.' To me this is an extremely 'fuzzy' and loose method of reasoning. It is taking the word 'myth' to apply to the Biblical attempt to explain and to interpret history by means of the God who by faith is known to reveal himself in history. That is something which the polytheist knows nothing about. It is not based on any feeling for the solidarity or 'the society of life' in nature, human society and the Divine. It rests on the attempt to take historical events seriously in the understanding that they are not self-explanatory but point to the active God behind them, who has set his love on man, the chief of his creatures, and has purposed to redeem him. If this is mythology, then how does one define the word? Can it be anything other than a term for faith which sees and portrays meaning beyond the empirical? If so, then it is nothing more than a synonym for faith or even religion. If this is the case, then what further use has the term for us except to infer that we no longer need take the Biblical presentation of history literally; either we must discard it as an outworn primitivism and discover its real meaning in an existential psychology, or we must read it solely as poetry.

This leads to a second objection to the use of the term 'mythology' for the Biblical theology of recital. The concentration is so much on the 'mythology' that history and historical research in the Bible are no longer important. All we need to do is to work with the 'mythology'; it makes no real difference whether the events really happened or not. How can one avoid a docetic view of the Bible in this case? Or if one tries to avoid docetism, will he not be tempted to turn from the Bible entirely to deal with other matters? In some theological quarters one gets the impression that the historical criticism of the Bible has left the faith on such shaky and unprovable historical foundations that we need to find another and firmer basis. Perhaps this exists in the investigation of being, of the Unconditioned, of the depth or the void (so, evidently, Paul Tillich).

Now in Biblical faith everything depends upon whether the central events actually occurred. Biblical scepticism might doubt whether God was the Director of the events (Jer. 5.12), but there was no doubt that there was an Exodus, that the nation was established at Mount Sinai, that it did obtain the land, that it did lose it subsequently, that Jesus did live, that he did die on a cross, and that he did appear subsequently to a large number of independent witnesses. These to the Biblical men are facts; the question is, What do they mean? To assume that it makes no difference whether they are facts or not is simply to destroy the whole basis of the faith. Or even to infer that these facts, if they are such, are irrelevant, would to the Biblical mind be a form of faithlessness or harlotry. Consequently, to the Biblical viewpoint it makes a great difference whether the events are really events or not. After all, to participate in Biblical faith means that we must indeed take history seriously as the primary data of the faith. By our historical research we discover errors and discrepancies, but this is a minor feature. The so-called destructive nature of Biblical criticism has been exaggerated and misrepresented. On the contrary, we today possess a greater confidence in the basic reliability of Biblical history, despite all the problems it has presented, than was possible before the historical criticism and archaeological research of the past century, and especially of the past three decades. Theologians, somewhat impatient with detailed historical work, find it simpler to assume that actually it is not especially important, except to add to the sum total of our antiquarian knowledge. Yet in any way to admit a disinterestedness in history or to assume it all to be mythical is certainly a strange way of dealing with Biblical theology, not to speak of the fact that it revives the ancient heresy of docetism.

On the other hand, it must be admitted that the Bible, while dealing with the facts of history in its own particular way, continually pushes beyond what is factually known because the knowledge of God leads both backward to creation and forward to the eschaton. Consequently, the farther back the Bible pushes, the more it is forced to use traditional material, rewritten to bring it into harmony with the author's purpose. Consequently, one cannot maintain the historical value of all parts evenly. But this situation is inevitable because the farther one moves from contemporary experience, the more he is dependent upon tradition. And when he reaches back to creation and forward to the end of current history, he must use symbols and pictures because he has no other means of presenting what he knows to be true. In this respect the current Bible-mythology school is certainly correct. Yet we should note that such Biblical projection is still presented in the manner of history, because it is indeed a projection from the known to that known alone by faith. Furthermore, all that the Biblical writers present they inevitably cast in terms of the world-view of their day. They knew nothing of limitless space; their universe was a comparatively small place surrounded by the watery deeps. The revelation of God occurred within the conceptual life of the people then. Yet the absence of a modern scientific view of the universe scarcely makes the literature in itself mythology.

Thus, if one must give a rational definition, it would appear that Biblical faith would better be designated as history interpreted by faith than as mythology. It is *itself*, unique, of its own kind; and the term 'mythology' confuses, rather than clarifies, this all-important fact. The church Father, Athanasius, in speaking of pagan mythology, remarks that the heathen make images because they are unable to conceive of God in terms higher than themselves, other creatures and 'irrational things'. There are learned men who explain that these visible gods are only to the end that the deity may answer them and be made manifest. Still others give deeper and more philosophical reasons. They say that the idols are for invocation and manifestation of divine angels and powers; by such means men are taught concerning the knowledge of God. They serve as letters to men, by referring to which men are taught to apprehend God. 'Such then is their mythology', Athanasius concludes, 'for far be it from us to call it theology.'[1] One has the suspicion that the current Bible-mythology school has been constructing arguments not totally dissimilar to those of the learned pagans. But if such is indeed mythology, far be it from us to call it the Biblical theology of recital.

[1] *Contra Gentes*, para. 19 (*Nicene and Post-Nicene Fathers*, Second Series, Vol. IV, p. 14). Reference given me by Professor Joseph Haroutunian.

INDEX OF BIBLICAL REFERENCES

OLD TESTAMENT

Index of Biblical References

Index of Biblical References

Index of Biblical References

NEW TESTAMENT